Traduzione

Vertimas raštu

Traduzzjoni

Tulkošana

ŷ

Vertaling

łumaczenia pisemne

Tradução

Traducere

Preklad

Prevajanje

Översättning

# Translation at the European Commission – a history

European
Commission

**Europe Direct is a service to help you find answers
to your questions about the European Union**

**Freephone number (*):**
**00 800 6 7 8 9 10 11**

(*) Certain mobile telephone operators do not allow access to 00 800 numbers or these
calls may be billed.

More information on the European Union is available on the Internet (http://europa.eu).

Cataloguing data can be found at the end of this publication.

The content of this publication does not necessarily reflect the position or views of the European Commission

Luxembourg: Office for Official Publications of the European Communities, 2010

ISBN 978-92-79-08849-0
doi: 10.2782/16417

*Printed in Spain*

PRINTED ON WHITE CHLORINE-FREE PAPER

# Acknowledgments

*In early 2008 the European Commission's Directorate-General for Translation decided to take stock of its first half-century of work. To put this into effect we consulted numerous sources of documentation, including of course the Commission's historical archives, and spoke to a hundred or so former and current members of the translation service and to representatives of other Directorates-General.*

*While writing the first draft we realised that this retrospective might be of interest to a wider audience than the Institution's staff alone. That is how this publication came about.*

*Our sincere thanks go to the archive team for its support and to our colleagues for their memories, their documents and their photographs. Without their help it would have been impossible to tell this captivating story.*

*This study is based essentially on information taken from historical and current Commission documents, but it also draws widely on the ideas and recollections of the interviewees.*

| | |
|---|---|
| Editor: | Audrey Pariente, Directorate-General for Translation |
| Project director: | Andrea Dahmen, Directorate-General for Translation |
| Editorial team: | Ioana Gligor, Tytti Granqvist, Philippe Marchetto, Luca Tomasi, Directorate-General for Translation |
| Translators (English version): | Christopher Birch, Barbara Hall, Brian Moon, Alan Morgan, Peter Workman, Directorate-General for Translation |
| Graphic design: | Publications Office |

December 2009

# Contents

# Symbols used

| Symbol | Meaning |
|---|---|
| 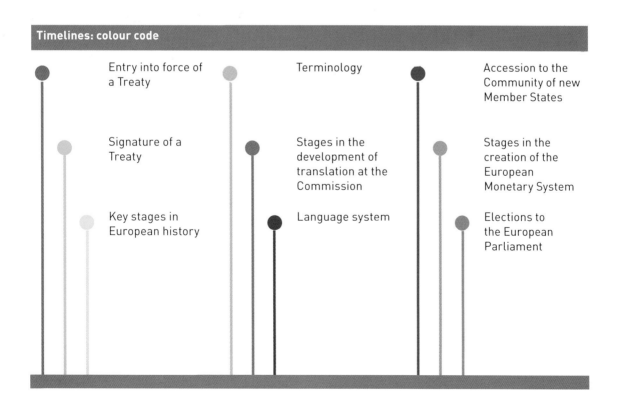 **Find out more?** | These boxes give further information and detail useful for understanding the text. |
| **DICAUTOM** | If a term is in bold blue type, it is further explained in the *Overview of Translation Tools* at the end of the volume (page 66). |
| *procedural languages* | If a term is in bold italics, it is defined in the *Glossary* at the end of the volume (page 72). |
| **CECA** | If an abbreviation is in bold orange type, the full name is given in the *List of abbreviations used* at the end of the volume (page 68). |

## Timelines: colour code

Entry into force of a Treaty

Terminology

Accession to the Community of new Member States

Signature of a Treaty

Stages in the development of translation at the Commission

Stages in the creation of the European Monetary System

Key stages in European history

Language system

Elections to the European Parliament

# Preface

THIS PUBLICATION IS the first attempt at tracing the development of the European Commission's translation service, from the days of the European Coal and Steel Community in the early 1950s to the modern-day European Union.

Far from being an end in itself, this history of the translation service is a crucial component of the European Union's institutional memory that demonstrates how multilingualism – one of its fundamental principles – was "translated" into action right from the start, long before it was formally established as a policy in its own right. By spotlighting the implications of certain decisions and marking out the twists and turns along the way, the story of the translation service also illuminates the path ahead.

The history of translation at the European Commission is first and foremost the story of the women and men whose work has helped to create the European Union. Union between the peoples of Europe would have been unthinkable without translation to build bridges. How, without translation, would nation states have reached agreement, and how would European citizens have played their part in realising such an ambitious project?

For over half a century these men and women have striven to put the European Union within the grasp of all its citizens. While Community multilingualism was needed originally as a pragmatic solution, today it is the vital element that makes the European Union unique. It has become a fundamental European principle, and translation plays a crucial role in respecting the European identity.

Over the past five decades translation has risen to many challenges by restructuring and becoming ever more innovative, keeping the Community machine running as smoothly with twenty-seven members as it did with six. The Commission's Directorate-General for Translation has proved itself capable of meeting every possible demand, and it will rise to the challenges of the future with the same competence and the same professionalism.

The multilingualism born with the Communities has made translation crucial to the building of Europe. Translators are the key that unlocks this tower of Babel. They contribute with modesty, courage and perseverance to the European ideal. They prove their talent and their creativity in expressing Community concepts in all European languages and disseminating the European message as widely as possible.

These are the considerations that led me to launch this publication. In the epic journey of the translators who, day after day, have given tangible expression to the dream of the founding fathers it is the full richness of the European tapestry that is revealed.

Enjoy!

Karl-Johan Lönnroth,
Director-General for Translation

Translation at the European Commission – a history

# The first two decades: the 1950s and 1960s

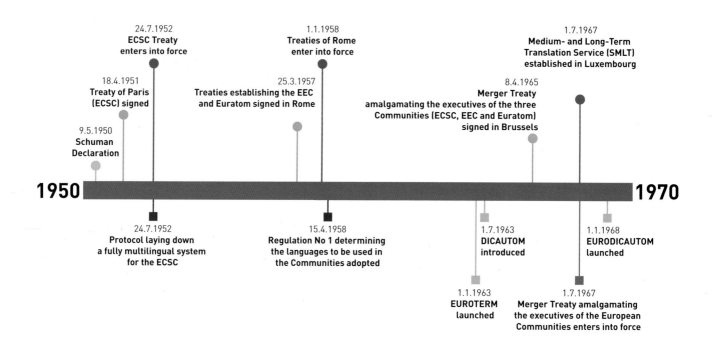

**24.7.1952**
ECSC Treaty
enters into force

**1.1.1958**
Treaties of Rome
enter into force

**1.7.1967**
Medium- and Long-Term
Translation Service (SMLT)
established in Luxembourg

**18.4.1951**
Treaty of Paris
(ECSC) signed

**25.3.1957**
Treaties establishing the EEC
and Euratom signed in Rome

**8.4.1965**
Merger Treaty
amalgamating the executives of the three
Communities (ECSC, EEC and Euratom)
signed in Brussels

**9.5.1950**
Schuman
Declaration

## 1950

## 1970

**24.7.1952**
Protocol laying down
a fully multilingual system
for the ECSC

**15.4.1958**
Regulation No 1 determining
the languages to be used in
the Communities adopted

**1.7.1963**
DICAUTOM
introduced

**1.1.1968**
EURODICAUTOM
launched

**1.1.1963**
EUROTERM
launched

**1.7.1967**
Merger Treaty amalgamating
the executives of the European
Communities enters into force

Timeline of the stages in building Europe, 1950-1970

FOLLOWING THE DEVASTATION brought by the Second World War, it was more vital than ever to forge an alliance between the peoples of Europe. On 9 May 1950 Robert Schuman, the French Minister for Foreign Affairs, suggested pooling the coal and steel resources of France, Germany and other countries wishing to help initiate economic cooperation and lay the foundations for a European federation. Thus he laid the first stone in the building of Europe.

Scarcely had they launched their bold project for putting political dialogue and economic cooperation in the place of supremacy theories and the roar of the canons, than the founding fathers of the European Community faced the choice of the language, or languages, to be used by the institutions in their daily activities, in relations with national authorities, foreign powers and private enterprise, and above all in communications with the people.

The gulf between the most bloody war in history and the pooling of economic resources by countries that are yesterday's enemies can clearly not be bridged by imposing the language of one of the partners on everyone else. Having only one official language was therefore never contemplated.

And a bilingual system based on the languages of the two main partners, French and German, would not have been compatible with Belgium's geopolitical situation, with the Dutch-speaking community claiming equal rights with the French speakers. And if Dutch were to be made an official language, Italian would of course also have to be one, having three times the number of speakers.

The language situation in the six founder countries thus answered the question of the *official languages* of the Community. In order to guarantee the right of every citizen to understand the provisions and measures

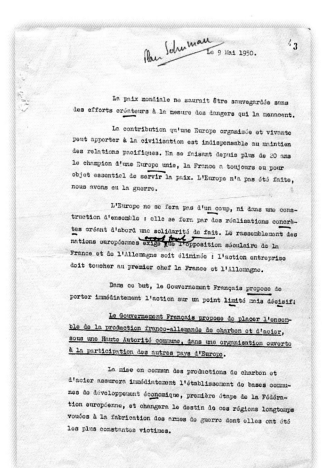

The Schuman Declaration (1950)

 **Find out more?**

*Luxembourgish is not one of the official Community languages, since it was not recognised as Luxembourg's 'national language' (alongside French and German) until 1984. The Grand-Duchy did not request its inclusion at that time. Luxembourg law is enacted in French, in line with the relevant legal provisions, which are in French.*

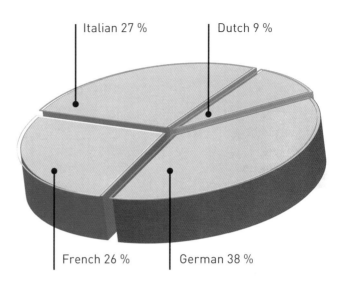

Italian 27 %    Dutch 9 %

French 26 %    German 38 %

Mother tongues of the citizens of the six founder countries (1951)

adopted by the Community and to acknowledge its linguistic and cultural differences, the Member States decided on four official languages for the Community: Dutch, French, German and Italian. The official languages of the six countries thus became official languages of the Community.

The multilingualism embraced from the start was thus a pragmatic solution rather than a political statement, since by adopting fewer languages the Community would have opened the door to new conflicts and lost the support of European citizens.

The Treaty of Paris establishing the European Coal and Steel Community (**ECSC**) was signed in 1951 by Belgium, France, Germany, Italy, Luxembourg and the Netherlands. The Treaty was drawn up in French, and the French version of the Treaty is the only authentic language version. The ECSC came into being in 1952 on the entry into force of the Treaty, which was concluded for a period of 50 years.

The Community was given several institutions. Its general interests were entrusted to a supranational collegiate executive body with nine members – the High Authority – assisted by a Consultative Committee representing producers, workers, consumers and dealers. The High Authority was overseen by a Common Assembly, a Court of Justice and a Special Council of Ministers. The Council represented the national governments, the Common Assembly consisted of 78 members designated by the national parliaments, and the

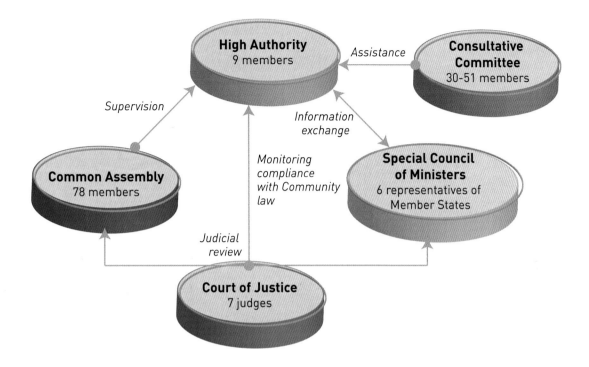

The ECSC Institutions (1951)

Court of Justice was established as an independent judiciary whose function was to ensure that Community law was observed.

The members of the Community as a whole decided to designate Luxembourg as the provisional place of work of the Institutions with the exception of the Assembly, which was based in both Luxembourg and Strasbourg. A protocol annexed to the Treaty called on the delegations to study in particular the question of the seat of the institutions and that of the *language system* of the Community and to make appropriate proposals to the governments.

In May 1951, just a few weeks after the Treaty was signed, a committee of legal experts met to examine the practices of international organisations in order to determine the language rules to be applied within the Community. Their conclusions pointed out that, though international precedents could provide models, it was essential to find new solutions suited specifically to the Community institutions. The committee stressed that the choice was essentially a pragmatic one: if those involved in the workings of the institutions were to be at ease and feel at home in this Community, then the languages spoken in the Member States must be used as widely as possible.

Once the members of the committee had reached agreement, a protocol was drawn up laying down the following language rules for the ECSC. The Community

### Find out more

*The international organisations whose practices were examined at that time were the* **UN**, *the* **OEEC**, *the* ***International Court of Justice***, *the* ***Council of Europe*** *and* **NATO**.

had four official languages. Decisions, recommendations, individual opinions and correspondence addressed to businesses were to be drawn up in the languages of the parties concerned. Correspondence addressed to the Community institutions was to be drawn up, at the discretion of the sender, in one of the official Community languages; the reply must be sent in the same language. The Assembly would itself decide on the practical questions of language use, with delegates able to choose between the four official languages of the Community. Lastly, the *Official Journal* (**OJ**) of the Community would have four editions, each in one of the four official languages.

From the very beginning, the Community's multilingualism has required professional linguists to ensure the smooth running and transparency of the Institutions' work and to give European citizens guaranteed access to their activities. Thus each Institution was equipped with a language service enabling it to meet its translation and interpretation needs.

It was only logical for the High Authority's language service to be organised by function: written requirements (translation department) and oral requirements (interpretation department). Its mission was to provide other departments, in good time, with the written or oral means of allowing the use of any of the official Community languages in their various activities.

A 1953 document from the High Authority refers to a total of 35 translators and *revisers* (10 revisers and 25 translators), divided into language sections. Right from the start there was an English section alongside the four official-language sections, since English was the language most widely used at international level by heavy industry, in the scientific and technical literature and in the coal and steel trade, particularly by the major British and American trading partners.

The German section had twelve translators, the French ten, the Dutch six, the Italian five and the English two. The translators of the High Authority's language service were assisted from time to time by external translators.

The language service formed part of the *'general' services* giving logistical support to the *'technical'*, and worked with the document reproduction service. The translators were assisted by a pool of stenographers, who took down the translations in shorthand, and of typists who typed them up. A planning office registered incoming and outgoing documents and monitored the progress of the translation and typing work. As regards recruitment, it was felt at the time that selecting translators was the job of the head of the service, who should be free to assess the applicants. Recruitment was not therefore based on competitions, but on admission tests organised on an *ad hoc* basis.

The increasing workflow very soon called for a rethink of the organisation and staffing of the language service. Internal memoranda flew back and forth between 1952 and 1957 as attempts were made to limit the workload under which the language service was struggling and to recruit new translators.

In 1955 the High Authority decided that strict rules were needed on the deadlines for the translation and reproduction of documents.

| Year | 1953 | 1954 | 1955 |
|---|---|---|---|
| Pages translated *(1 page = 1 500 characters not counting spaces)* | 38 855 | 57 295 | 61 568 |

The first production statistics

To allow the language service to cope with demand and deliver texts on time, including the clean typing of the finished product, requesting departments would be subject to greater discipline with regard both to deadlines and to the length of texts for translation.

At that time different departments were involved in translation, reproduction and dissemination. First there was the documentation department, which received the original text in one of the four official Community languages and sent it to the language service. The translation deadline was fixed by agreement between the documentation and language services in the light of the volume of work in progress and the number of translators available. When the job was completed, the translated text was returned to the documentation service registry, which sent it to the typing pool for clean typing (with carbon copies or on duplicator stencils) and proofreading.

The capacity (or throughput) of the language service was measured at that time in pages per day or per hour. It depended essentially on the number of translators and revisers and, to a lesser extent, on the difficulty of the texts.

An internal High Authority document of that same year also points out that the calculations must take into account two elements that could slow down the work: the near impossibility of translating directly from Dutch to Italian and vice versa, and the shortage of typists. With these reservations the writer states that, per typed page of thirty or so lines, some forty minutes must be allowed for a rough translation and one hour for a revised text.

According to the same report, after four years of practical experience it was time to rationalise the organisation. The measures to be taken should link together hitherto separate operations in order to achieve work continuity, coordinate the efforts of the staff, meet the service's commitments to requesters and avoid, or at least limit, idle periods. The

**Find out more?**

*In 1956 the High Authority specified that documents intended for the Council, like internal documents, would usually be drawn up only in German and French, but that, unless otherwise stated, all documents for the Assembly or the Consultative Committee must be prepared in all four Community languages. The translation and reproduction of documents for the Council, the Assembly and the Consultative Committee would take general priority and must be completed within forty-eight hours.*

document put forward a solution to these problems. First it recommended boosting the staff of the language service by establishing a table of theoretically essential posts and rapidly recruiting permanent staff in order to avoid, at normal times, the use of temporary translators, which involved greater expense for the same productivity. It next recommended putting most of the typing pool under the control of the language service for work purposes (dictation, typing and proofreading). Lastly it suggested attaching the documentation service registry to the language service. The creation of a central terminology and research office to standardise vocabulary and avoid multiple translations of identical terms was mentioned for the first time.

Until 1957 the ECSC language arrangements were defined in various protocols and reports, and although the language system was implicitly regulated there were no specific rules in force. The exchanges of memoranda and the problems encountered up to then in the functioning of the language service led the High Authority to adopt, in 1957, an internal agreement setting out the approach to be followed to resolve the situation. First, requests for translation into Dutch, German, Italian and English must be reduced to a strict minimum (French was generally the language of the original). Secondly, the divisions (or technical departments) themselves were asked to carry out less important translations, since their staff were expected on recruitment to speak at least one official Community language in addition to their mother tongue. They were also asked to reduce as far as possible the length of texts for translation by the language service. Lastly, they were called on to schedule meetings requiring translation work only after receiving a guarantee from the head of the language service that the documents could be delivered by the desired date. These measures were intended as a temporary solution to the language-service overload.

Following the successful bringing together of the Six in the ECSC, the founding States of Europe decided to take European cooperation a step further.

In 1957 the Treaties of Rome establishing the European Economic Community (**EEC**) and the European Atomic Energy Community (**EAEC/Euratom**) were signed by Belgium, France, Germany, Italy, Luxembourg and the Netherlands, and they entered into force in 1958. The Treaties were drawn up in all four official Community languages, each language version being authentic. The main purpose of the EEC Treaty was to establish a **common market** within which goods would move freely. The **EURATOM** Treaty was initially created to coordinate the Member States' research programmes with a view to the peaceful use of nuclear energy.

These two Communities, like the ECSC, had several institutions — five in total: a Commission consisting of nine members for the EEC and five for Euratom, an Assembly of 142 members, a Council consisting of six representatives of the Member States, an Economic and Social Committee of 101 members, and a Court of Justice consisting of seven judges and two advocates-general. The three Communities shared the Court of Justice and the Assembly. The Commissions of the two new Communities were provisionally based in Brussels.

Following the entry into force of the Treaties of Rome, the need to regulate the use of languages within the Communities meant drawing up rules governing the language arrangements of the EEC and of Euratom: in both cases this led to Regulation No 1 of 1958. The terms of the two Regulations were the same. The Council, acting unanimously, established the language system of the Communities' Institutions. Until these Regulations were adopted, the language system was codified only in various reports and protocols. The Regulations enacted the system with which the Communities were to comply. They were based on the protocol on the language system in the ECSC and laid down the same operating rules as for the ECSC.

Signing of the Treaties of Rome, 25 March 1957

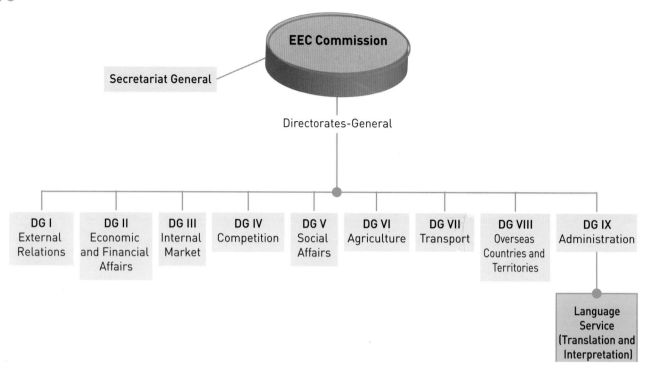

Departments of the EEC Commission in 1959

Article 1 of the Regulations lists the official languages of the Communities (four in 1958). Under Article 2, documents which a Member State or a person subject to the jurisdiction of a Member State sends to institutions of the Community may be in any one of the official languages, and the reply must be drafted in the same language, while under Article 3 documents which an institution sends to a Member State or to a person subject to the jurisdiction of a Member State must be in the language of that State. Article 4 provides for documents of general application to be drafted in the four official languages. Article 5 provides for the *Official Journal of the Communities* to be published in the four official languages. Article 6 entitles the Institutions to stipulate in their rules of procedure which of the languages are to be used in specific cases.

The originality of these arrangements for the operation of the Communities made translation essential to protect the rights of European citizens. The Commission of each Community therefore set up its own language service to provide the translations required. The organisation of the language services of the Commissions of the EEC and Euratom was at first based on the same model as that of the ECSC High Authority. The language service was part of the personnel and administration division and was responsible for both translation and interpretation

So on the entry into force of the Treaties, the Euratom and EEC Commissions were set up in Brussels. A Head of Division was in charge of the language services, which were made up of five language groups (the four official languages plus English). Each group was assisted by a secretariat and typing pool. Each of the four groups working into the official Community languages (Dutch, French, German and Italian) had about ten translators. One English translator, quickly followed by two more, was hired from the start, as had been the case with the ECSC, to handle communications with the United States, the United Kingdom and the largely English-dominated international scientific research community. The Euratom and EEC translators translated into their mother tongues — and very rarely in the other direction. Subject knowledge was often more important than foreign-language expertise, and experts in a field were always on hand to explain a technical term or help linguists to find the ideal translation. If they knew the subject, therefore, translators were willing to translate even documents in languages they knew less well.

In the early 1960s the language services of the three Communities each had some fifty translators. The Euratom language service was far too small to cope with the volume of pages to be translated, and new posts had to be fought for. There were no entrance competitions: as soon as posts became vacant, the established translators looked for competent applicants to take admission tests. The successful candidates were appointed.

At this time, translators would work on mechanical typewriters or dictate their text directly to a typist. The text was edited by a reviser and returned to the typist for a clean copy to be produced. Secretaries corrected *stencils* with the help of a red liquid that hardened to form a film over the error. From the mid-1960s onwards, translators worked with dictaphones which recorded the translations on plastic discs; these were huge, cumbersome machines, but were more robust and reliable than the magnetic tapes that replaced them later.

In 1962 new internal rules on translation appeared at the EEC. The purpose was to codify and supplement the measures concerning translation laid down since July 1958 in various internal memoranda. These rules standardised the work of the language service. They firstly addressed the nature of the work and distinguished between texts for translation only (in draft form) and texts to be both translated and reproduced. Secondly, the procedure to be followed when requesting a translation was set out. Any request for translation or reproduction was to be sent to the planning office, which would register the document and give it a reference number. The request was then sent to the language service; afterwards the translation was returned to the planning office, which sent it on to the

**Find out more?**

*Stencils were sheets of waxed paper perforated by the impact of typewriter characters and used as a matrix for printing several copies of a document.*

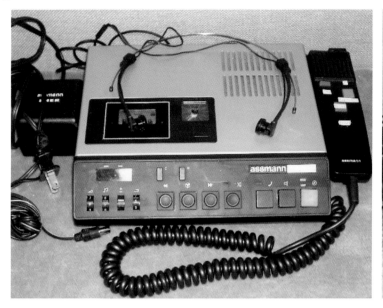
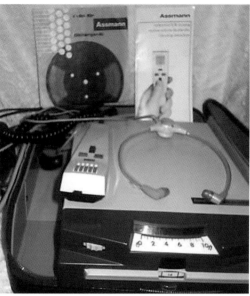

Two generations of Assmann dictaphones

requester. In the same year the status of permanent official laid down in the Protocol on the Privileges and Immunities of the European Communities annexed to the Treaty of Rome was finalised. Although the United Kingdom was not part of the Community, the English-language translators also became permanent officials.

In the mid-1960s the leaders of the Member States contemplated centralising the work of the Institutions of the Communities to improve the efficiency of their decision-making processes. It was therefore decided to merge the executive bodies of the Communities.

The Merger Treaty amalgamating the executives of the three Communities (Treaty of Brussels) was signed in Brussels on 8 April 1965 by Belgium, France, Germany, Italy, Luxembourg and the Netherlands and entered into force on 1 July 1967. This Treaty merged the executive structures put in place by the EEC, ECSC and Euratom Treaties. The three Communities already shared the **Court of Justice** and the **Parliament**. The Treaty instituted a single **Council of the European Communities** and a single Commission of the European Communities (formerly known as the High Authority in the ECSC context). These Institutions now shared the same budget and were based in Brussels. The plural term *Communities* also made its appearance at this time.

The merger of the executive structures of the three Communities brought with it a major reorganisation of departments, which were divided between Brussels and Luxembourg. The new Commission had departments in both cities. The departments in Luxembourg were the heirs to the ECSC departments, while those in Brussels consisted of the former Euratom and EEC staff.

In Brussels, the Euratom and EEC language services were amalgamated into a single language service belonging to the Commission of the European Communities. Although the merger was effective on paper as from 1967, Euratom's language service remained separate from that of the EEC until 1973. The two departments nevertheless shared a building. It was not until after the 1973 accession and the arrival of new Danish, English and Irish translators that the two language services of the EEC and Euratom truly became one. There was now a single head of division in charge of all Commission translators in Brussels.

In Luxembourg, a Medium- and Long-Term Translation Service (SMLT) was set up in 1967 to take on most of the work formerly done by the High Authority's translation service. This service translated the technical documents associated with the activities of the ECSC and the other Luxembourg-based Commission departments. It also translated public invitations to tender for publication in the Official Journal. An Office for Official Publications of the European Communities (OPOCE) came into being in the same period and took responsibility for all the Communities' publications. A Joint Sales Office was attached to it. The following Commission departments were also based in Luxembourg, at first provisionally: the Statistical Office, the data processing department (processing statistical data on punch cards), the EEC and ECSC occupational health and safety departments, the Directorate-General for the Dissemination of Information, the Directorate for Health Protection and the Euratom Safeguards Directorate. The governments of the Member States were willing to establish other Community agencies and departments, particularly in the financial field, in Luxembourg or to transfer them there, provided that their smooth operation was guaranteed.

As early as 1968, thought was given to upgrading both the profession of translator and the language service itself. The idea was to turn the translation service into an autonomous body, raise the profile of the reviser's job, create specialist multilingual groups and strengthen the authority of the planning department *vis-à-vis* the requester departments. The translators consulted on the restructuring of the service generally favoured organisation by language, and it was this solution that was chosen. The service also set up groups of specialist translators within the language sections so as to encourage familiarity with the subject-matter and thus improve translation quality and productivity. At the same time the translators set up their own Permanent Delegation of Translators (DPT). The DPT saw the light of day on 13 June 1968 as the outcome of a general assembly which prepared the ground for a working party to examine the reorganisation of the translation services. As the representative body for a specific profession (and function), the DPT was a new departure within the Commission, even though temporary delegations had occasionally been formed to solve problems specific to certain jobs or categories.

Community cooperation was proving successful and the Member States soon contemplated taking it still further. Although the United Kingdom, Ireland, Denmark and Norway had applied to join the Communities as early as 1961, it was not until the 1970s that the six founder countries envisaged widening their circle. Accession negotiations were launched at that time, which for the Commission's language service meant translating official texts into the languages of the future Member States. At the time of an enlargement, the translation service is one of the first Commission departments to be called upon. It is without doubt the department with the heaviest burden, not only in the final phase before an accession, since it is responsible for the revision of **secondary legislation** translated in the countries awaiting accession, but also in the initial phase after accession, since all relevant legislative acts must be available in all languages as from day one. Candidate countries thus translate the **Community acquis** into their languages with the help of the staff of the Community Institutions, who explain to them legal terms that are new to them and unfamiliar legal concepts found in Community jargon. Translating the *acquis* demands a major research effort and the creation of a large body of new terminology.

# Terminology at the Commission

THE ROLE OF TRANSLATORS within the Community ambit is important in that they participate in the exercise of public authority. Translation is a service responsible for ensuring communication between the different departments of the institution. Translators have to be versatile, particularly as regards the translation of the major treaties. They are expected to translate anything whenever needed. Much of their energy is accordingly devoted to terminological research. The increasing need for translation, and thus for translators, generates a corresponding need for terminology in order to facilitate the task of translation. During the 1960s, ever tighter deadlines and the technical nature of the texts, sometimes

beyond the capacity of the linguists, prompted translators to entrust part of their research work to other colleagues. This is how the the High Authority's first terminologists emerged.

In 1964 the High Authority used terminologists *inter alia* to harmonise legal vocabulary, their role being to list complete phrases corresponding to legal situations. The work of the terminologists made it possible to give everyone the benefit of pooled individual efforts. The translation services of the Commissions and the High Authority also set up terminology units to support translators in their quest for equivalences. Ad hoc research, first in two languages, was extended to the four languages, then published in bulletins produced by the different terminology services of the institutions. The work very quickly led to the production of multilingual lists, e.g. collections, lexicons, glossaries and vocabulary lists.

The Euratom Commission for its part undertook to standardise terminology in the nuclear domain. Article 8 of the Euratom Treaty indeed states that Euratom '… shall also ensure that a uniform nuclear terminology and a standard system of measurements are established'. This can be considered as the birth of European terminology in an international treaty. It was only with the merger of the executive bodies of the three Communities that the terminology services came to form a single service. The periodical *Terminologie et traduction* (T&T) was born out of this, taking over from the terminology bulletins formerly published independently of one another.

At the Commission, terminology was the guarantee of equivalence between the languages used. Until 2002 all the Commission's terminologists were grouped together in one big terminology unit. They had a specialist library containing the books and documentation they needed for their research work and a full set of Community glossaries. The 2002 restructuring exercise dismantled the terminology unit and the T&T periodical was discontinued.

The doubling of the number of official languages in the wake of the 2004 enlargement brought fresh challenges. The mountain of information available in the 'old' languages made it imperative for a team to sift through and manage the data, deciding which concepts should be used and which avoided. Consolidating the information was a monumental task. The problem was different for the new languages. While the old languages buckled under a wealth of resources the new languages suffered cruelly from a shortage of data. Whence a twofold problem: the need on the one hand to consolidate the data in the old languages and on the other to seek out, create and make available to translators and other users terminology in the new languages. In 2004, this situation prompted a rethink of the dismantling of the terminology unit and reinstatement of a sector to be responsible for coordinating terminological work carried out in the translation units.

The new technologies available enabled translators to locate large quantities of information using the Internet, which meant they no longer needed terminologists to the same extent. However, while the number of questions might admittedly have declined, at the same time they were more difficult and specific, as they related to terms which the translators had been unable to find elsewhere. Working methods were strongly influenced by the tools which had become available. The issue of cost was a major consideration. Maintaining a comprehensive documentary and terminological infrastructure was expensive, and the new facilities available called into question the whole point of a terminology service. It was therefore imperative at this juncture to properly define the function of terminologists in order to justify their existence.

# The 1970s and 1980s

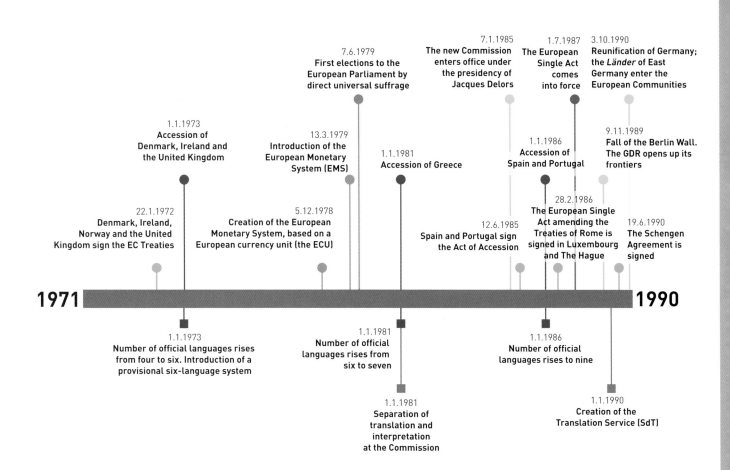

**7.6.1979**
First elections to the
European Parliament by
direct universal suffrage

**7.1.1985**
The new Commission
enters office under
the presidency of
Jacques Delors

**1.7.1987**
The European
Single Act
comes
into force

**3.10.1990**
Reunification of Germany;
the *Länder* of East
Germany enter the
European Communities

**1.1.1973**
Accession of
Denmark, Ireland and
the United Kingdom

**13.3.1979**
Introduction of the
European Monetary
System (EMS)

**1.1.1981**
Accession of Greece

**1.1.1986**
Accession of
Spain and Portugal

**9.11.1989**
Fall of the Berlin Wall.
The GDR opens up its
frontiers

**22.1.1972**
Denmark, Ireland,
Norway and the United
Kingdom sign the EC Treaties

**5.12.1978**
Creation of the European
Monetary System, based on a
European currency unit (the ECU)

**12.6.1985**
Spain and Portugal sign
the Act of Accession

**28.2.1986**
The European Single
Act amending the
Treaties of Rome is
signed in Luxembourg
and The Hague

**19.6.1990**
The Schengen
Agreement is
signed

**1971**                                                                **1990**

**1.1.1973**
Number of official languages rises
from four to six. Introduction of a
provisional six-language system

**1.1.1981**
Number of official
languages rises from
six to seven

**1.1.1986**
Number of official
languages rises to nine

**1.1.1981**
Separation of
translation and
interpretation
at the Commission

**1.1.1990**
Creation of the
Translation Service (SdT)

Timeline of the stages in building Europe, 1971 – 1990

In 1971, the Commission transmitted to the Council the first full text in English of the ECSC Treaty and its Annexes I to III, along with the Treaties establishing the European Economic Community (EEC) and the European Atomic Energy Community, to which the representatives of the Commission and those of the United Kingdom and of Ireland had given their agreement. The amendments stemming from the Merger Treaty of 8 April 1965 were included in these texts.

Moreover, the Irish government wanted Irish to be recognised as an official language of the enlarged Community. It was nonetheless agreed that the use of Irish in the Community context would be limited to translation of the instruments relating to accession, but without the provisions of secondary legislation, and to the translation of the Treaties establishing the ECSC, the EEC and Euratom. The number of other Community texts to be drawn up in Irish was to be limited. The Community thus accepted Irish as a treaty language of the enlarged Community, on the understanding that this did not imply the introduction of Irish as a working language of the European institutions.

From the end of 1970, the Commission recruited teams of language revisers for Danish and Norwegian with a view to preparing the Danish and Norwegian texts of the Treaties. The translation work began in 1971 (for accession scheduled for 1973). The team of Danish language revisers was given the task of preparing the Danish text of the Merger Treaty of 8 April 1965 and related documents, and also the Treaty of 22 April 1970 amending certain budgetary provisions of the Treaties establishing the European Communities.

In 1971 and 1972, the team of Norwegian language revisers had the task of preparing the Norwegian versions of the Merger Treaty, the Treaty establishing the EAEC, and the annexes to the EEC Treaty. This ambitious task undertaken by the Communities culminated in 1973 with the accession of the United Kingdom, of Ireland and of Denmark. Norway did not join the Communities because of the 'no' vote in the referendum on membership.

The accession in 1973 of three new Member States brought certain changes in the organisation of the language service. It remained part of the "Personnel and administration" Directorate-General. The Brussels department was part of Directorate D "Translation, documentation, reproduction, library". In Luxembourg there was still the Medium and Long-term Translation Service (SMLT). The structure remained unchanged until the early 1980s, the only notable development being the setting up of a service for coordinating and preparing publications. In 1981, following a huge amount of preparatory work and a 'yes' vote in the referendum on membership, Greece joined the European Communities.

Until the mid-1980s the language service, still attached to the Directorate-General for Personnel and Administration, was divided into two separate parts, one in Brussels and the other in Luxembourg. The importance of translation grew over the years, which led the Commission to reconsider the status of the service. Accordingly, at the end of 1985, translation was made into a single department headed by a director. At this point, there were 955 translators.

The tasks carried out by the service diversified in the wake of the signature in Luxembourg in February 1986 of the Single European Act, which ushered in new policies while at the same time strengthening certain provisions of the Treaties of Rome. The Single Act came into force on 1 July 1987, its name deriving from the fact that for the first time in a treaty there were simultaneously Community provisions (supranational level) and intergovernmental provisions (international level). It was the product of the resolve of Jacques Delors, then President of the European Commission, to give fresh impetus to European integration after the period of 'euroscepticism' which followed the oil shock of the 1970s. The Single Act brought changes to the Treaty establishing the EEC, developing its objectives and paving the way for the single market. It set the objective for the end of 1992 of completing the single market, defined as 'an area without internal frontiers in which the free movement of goods, persons, services and capital is ensured in accordance with the provisions of this Treaty'. The Single Act broadened the responsibilities of the EEC in three main areas: research and technological development, the environment and the common foreign policy. It strengthened the powers of the European Parliament, allowed the Council to create the Court of First Instance and cemented the existence of the European Council.

# The translation service's premises in Brussels and Luxembourg

JECL building, seen from *rue de la Joyeuse Entrée*

ONE OF THE recurring demands of translators is proximity to the other Commission departments. The translators have been moved around time and again and the history of the premises they have occupied is a saga in itself.

In Brussels, the translation service was split between a variety of premises scattered across the city before being brought together at the beginning of the 1990s in a single building, the JECL. Located in the heart of the European district, it was situated at the nerve centre of the institutions and was ideally placed for following the life of the city of Brussels. From the offices facing *rue de la Loi*, it was possible to follow European and Belgian affairs through the various events and demonstrations taking place. Nevertheless, while having undeniable advantages, it was by then one of the oldest buildings occupied by the Commission.

At the end of 1997 there was a meeting to take stock of the state of the JECL building and assess the work needed to renovate it. The solutions envisaged included moving the translation service to a new site. Three sites were compatible with the needs of the service, but despite the advantages offered by certain options, the translators refused to move. An interim solution nevertheless had to be found, as the poor state of repair of the building had become a serious concern and the prevailing conditions hampered the work of the people housed there. In 2004 it was decided, in agreement with the owner of the premises, that all the offices would be renovated. However, despite this work, the JECL still remained a very old building. A final solution was therefore imposed: a move to *rue de Genève*, a location far from the life of the institutions and not amenable to the translators. The offices of DGT were moved to *rue de Genève* between March and the summer of 2006.

Demolition of the JECL building

In Luxembourg, until the Jean Monnet building (JMO) was opened in 1975 on the Kirchberg plateau, the accommodation of the translation units was also rather complicated. The main problem was to maintain the cohesion of the language groups in premises which were ill-adapted and shared by various Commission departments.

By contrast, in the Jean Monnet building, which housed all the Commission departments (with the exception of the Publications Office), being close to the requesting departments was ideal. The provisional installation of Commission departments in Luxembourg, as decided by a protocol annexed to the Merger Treaty of 8 April 1965, was confirmed by the Edinburgh European Council of 12 December 1992. In February 2003, after a thorough examination of its tasks and resources, the Commission decided to consolidate its departments in Luxembourg. In particular, it increased by 460 the number of translation posts for the languages of the new Member States. This decision came in response to Luxembourg's misgivings over the perceived trend towards centralisation of the Commission's departments in Brussels. The new staff were all housed in the JMO. This steel-structured building of 100 000 m² housed to the ECSC

The JMO building, Kirchberg

Consultative Committee until 2002 (when the Treaty of Paris expired), together with the part of the Publications Office and DGT. It was also for a long time home to the Statistical Office (Eurostat). However, the building has aged and it is now necessary to look towards its replacement. Owing to lack of space certain departments have been re-accommodated in premises scattered across the city. DGs **TREN**, **SANCO** and **ADMIN** have left the JMO and its vicinity. In 2009 it was decided that the JMO would be demolished and a new centre built in two phases to accommodate all the Commission's departments in Luxembourg.

The JMO building

The history of the translation service also took a decisive turn under the presidency of Jacques Delors. An incident which placed translators in the limelight occurred in 1986. At the time there were plans to move the translators to a more modern building, but one that was not in the centre and far from the rest of the Commission's buildings. This did not go down well with the translators, who went on strike and threatened to continue strike action until their demands were met. The strike temporarily brought the work of the Commission to a standstill. Jacques Delors reacted strongly to the threat of further strike action, which could completely paralyse the Commission's work. He therefore decided to take action to prevent the system from grinding to a halt. Accordingly, in 1989, he separated off the language service from the Directorate-General for Personnel and Administration, elevating it to the status of independent service headed by a Director-General. Its official title was henceforth that of "Translation Service" (**SdT**). Edouard Brackeniers was appointed head of the service, with the task of overhauling it and bringing home to the translators that they were an integral part of the functioning of the Commission, so as to head off further strike action and ensure the productivity of the service. The Director-General also obtained assurances that all the Brussels-based translation staff would be housed in a single building in the heart of the European district.

The main difference this change brought to translation was greater recognition of the profession of translator. Henceforth part of an independent service, translators saw the status of their function reinforced and now felt themselves to be on an equal footing with other Community officials. In addition, the work of translation was no longer solely to serve other Directorates General, but was recognised as an integral part of the European Commission's decision-making process.

Upon his arrival, the Director-General sought the advice of his immediate colleagues to decide how best to fulfil his mission. As a first step, he decided that the structure of the service, until then organised by language groups, needed to be changed. Accordingly, he set up thematic groups in order to organise translation work on the basis of the requesting departments. At the time the new structure offered greater transparency and enabled the requesting departments to better understand how the translation service worked and to get a response better tailored to their needs. Seven thematic departments were set up, each working on sectoral policies. They were subdivided into language units with between 10 and 25 translators and three to five secretaries. There were some 90 translators per language, with the exception of the *procedural languages* (English, French and German), for which the numbers were higher. This rationalisation of work enhanced the specialisation of translators, making for higher productivity and closer contact with the requesting departments. The key feature of the system was the thematic adviser managing his/her department with the assistance of a planning unit. The thematic adviser negotiated deadlines with the various departments, organised quality control and promoted the organisation of specialised teams. The thematic approach was a response to one of the weaknesses of the former system, i.e. the lack of synchronisation and coordination between the language groups. The work of the Commission had occasionally been held up because of delays in one or more language versions becoming available. As all the language versions are needed to launch the *interinstitutional procedure*, these delays could bring the Community legislative process to a standstill.

Nevertheless, the Director-General did not do away with language-based organisation altogether. He kept documentation centres for each language and created the function of language coordinator to manage the language-related problems encountered by the translators of the same language group. Working in conjunction with the Resources Unit, the language coordinator also took on a range of administrative functions with regard to the recruitment of translators and the selection of trainees. The language coordinators played an essential role in language-related disputes. Certain dossiers threw up problems for all languages, and the coordinators helped to find solutions to tricky problems. Generally speaking, the new structure was conducive to greater contact between the different nationalities and languages within the thematic groups. Concordance meetings were held at which translators from different language units discussed the problems they came across when translating documents from the same source language. Problems could thus be solved more rapidly and harmonisation across the different languages was enhanced.

# The 1990s and 2000s

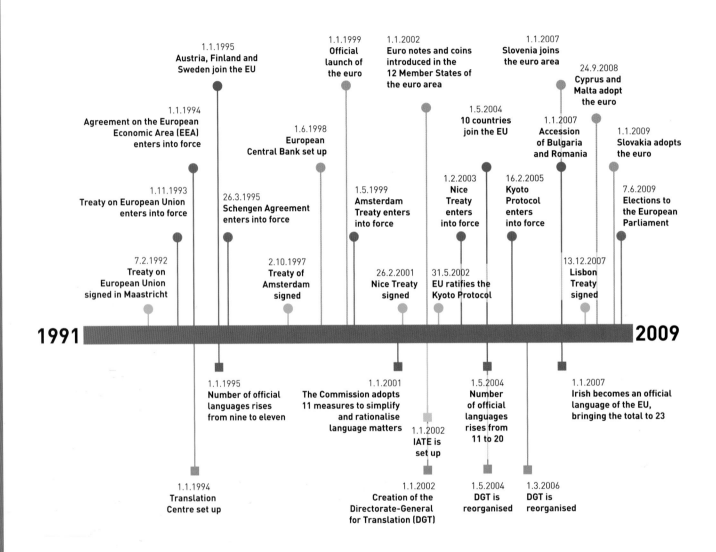

**1.1.1995**
Austria, Finland and
Sweden join the EU

**1.1.1999**
Official
launch of
the euro

**1.1.2002**
Euro notes and coins
introduced in the
12 Member States of
the euro area

**1.1.2007**
Slovenia joins
the euro area

**24.9.2008**
Cyprus and
Malta adopt
the euro

**1.1.1994**
Agreement on the European
Economic Area (EEA)
enters into force

**1.6.1998**
European
Central Bank set up

**1.5.2004**
10 countries
join the EU

**1.1.2007**
Accession
of Bulgaria
and Romania

**1.1.2009**
Slovakia adopts
the euro

**1.11.1993**
Treaty on European Union
enters into force

**26.3.1995**
Schengen Agreement
enters into force

**1.5.1999**
Amsterdam
Treaty enters
into force

**1.2.2003**
Nice
Treaty
enters
into force

**16.2.2005**
Kyoto
Protocol
enters
into force

**7.6.2009**
Elections to
the European
Parliament

**7.2.1992**
Treaty on
European Union
signed in Maastricht

**2.10.1997**
Treaty of
Amsterdam
signed

**26.2.2001**
Nice Treaty
signed

**31.5.2002**
EU ratifies the
Kyoto Protocol

**13.12.2007**
Lisbon
Treaty
signed

**1991** | **2009**

**1.1.1995**
Number of official
languages rises
from nine to eleven

**1.1.2001**
The Commission adopts
11 measures to simplify
and rationalise
language matters

**1.5.2004**
Number
of official
languages
rises from
11 to 20

**1.1.2007**
Irish becomes an official
language of the EU,
bringing the total to 23

**1.1.2002**
IATE is
set up

**1.1.1994**
Translation
Centre set up

**1.1.2002**
Creation of the
Directorate-General
for Translation (DGT)

**1.5.2004**
DGT is
reorganised

**1.3.2006**
DGT is
reorganised

Timeline of the stages in building Europe, 1991 – 2009

The 1990s saw major developments in European integration. On 7 February 1992 in Maastricht, the Member States of the EEC signed a treaty reforming the functioning of the Community. This was the Treaty on European Union (TEU), commonly known as the Maastricht Treaty, which established the European Union, founded on three 'pillars': the European Communities, the common foreign and security policy (CFSP), and police and police and judicial cooperation in criminal matters. This Treaty also provided the European Council with an institutional framework, established European citizenship and strengthened the powers of the European Parliament. In addition, it launched Economic and Monetary Union (EMU), which was to culminate with the introduction of the euro.

These new policies entailed considerable translation and terminological research work for the SdT. Translation demand within the Commission rose sharply, fuelled by the dynamic activity of the departments responsible for the single market and the new policy areas (trans-European networks, consumer protection, education and vocational training, youth-related matters, culture, development cooperation). In 1991 the service conducted a survey to find ways of managing demand. A number of steps were taken: raising awareness among the requesting departments, diversifying the range of services provided (e.g. summaries, oral translation, post-editing of machine translation) and outsourcing translation work. This latter step raised misgivings amongst translators, who feared a probable decline in quality and were wary of the risk of 'privatisation' of the service. Another option was to assign translators to various departments, the underlying idea being that such secondment would offer proximity to the requesters and thus increase efficiency. The idea was examined but the project was eventually dropped.

These structural changes and the introduction of information technology led to considerable changes in the working methods of the service. Translators became increasingly autonomous, and the age of the typing pool was well and truly over. These changes led to discussions within the Commission on the way forward for the profession of secretary, which had become so much more diversified since the time of the typing pool, particularly with the generalisation of computer tools and office technology.

# The secretary's role

THE JOB OF secretary has changed considerably since the 1950s. Secretaries, at the time referred to as typists or shorthand typists, then worked in pools. The work itself was rather mechanical, and the jobs were mainly held by women. In the language service, their role was to type the texts dictated by the translators.

In the 1970s, each language group had its own typing pool comprising some 30 secretaries divided into two groups, one group for clean typing and one for rough typing. They all worked in the same room separated into two parts by the office – a sort of glass cage – of the head of the pool.

At first, the secretaries rough-typed texts dictated on large discs with a diameter of approximately 30 cm (the Dictorel, which was the Commission translators' main working tool until 1979), and after that on mini tape cassettes with a recording capacity of about 15 minutes. Once the rough version had been corrected by the translator, the text was handed over to the reviser for re-reading before being returned, complete with stick-on strips used to make corrections, for clean-typing. However, the language service in Brussels gradually stopped providing systematic clean-typing, and the revised and corrected rough versions of the translations were sent directly to the requester. In Luxembourg, the language service had never provided a clean-typing service except exceptionally when asked for by the requester. The translation, as initially corrected on multiple-layer NCR paper, was sent to the requester along with one of the four handwritten copies of the job sheet ("fiche de travail").

When the language service was overhauled in 1989, the typing pools disappeared and the role of secretary was redefined. The function of unit secretary was created and systematised in the mid-1990s as part of the overall effort to attain the objectives of the language units.

Secretaries worked on all sorts of machines: first on mechanical typewriters and then on automatic typewriters. Documents had to be returned in all languages in a single format with the same number of pages. This caused problems and became a major constraint when, for instance, there were tables.

The slightest mistake in one table meant having to restart the typing all over again.

Stencils disappeared at the start of the 1990s. They were used at the time mainly for the reproduction of long documents (e.g. the General Report) on a Roneo machine. The black sheet had to be corrected using a red correcting fluid, the page being read against the light. The secretaries later worked on terminals before the arrival of PCs, at which point secretarial work underwent a radical change, as the computer gave the translators a far higher degree of autonomy by enabling them to input their translations themselves. With the resulting reduction in typing work, the typist-secretary has virtually disappeared.

Very few translators now use a dictating machine, and the function of secretary is now more akin to that of an assistant. The secretary is now a key element in the communication chain and assists the unit's translators, inter alia by preparing documents for translation, gathering reference material and pre-processing documents using systems for computer-assisted translation. The secretary books in and sends out documents and keeps the workflow monitoring system up to date. In addition, secretaries check that the format of translations corresponds in all respects to that of the original. Until the 1990s, secretarial posts were generally occupied by women, but they are now increasingly open to men.

At the start of the decade, the work of the service was also marked by the translation and revision of texts comprising the *acquis communautaire* in the run-up to the accession of Austria, Finland, Sweden and Norway. Mindful of the lessons learned during previous enlargements, the translation service looked at new ways of meeting this fresh challenge. A group of Brussels-based translators and revisers was set up, reporting to the Director-General and tasked with coordinating the translation and revision work carried out in the candidate countries. At the same time, temporary staff were recruited to revise the acquis communautaire in the capitals of the candidate countries.

The Finns opted to translate the acquis communautaire from the French version, drawing heavily on national legal experts, while the Swedes chose to work from the English version.

This organisational approach enabled the candidate countries, when referendum time came around, to have the translations of the *acquis* ready and available. Accordingly, the candidate countries, with the exception of Norway, where for the second time the referendum went against membership, joined the European Union in 1995. Following accession, special arrangements for translation work were granted to the Finnish and Swedish units in order to allow a gradual transition until they had the same number of translators as the other language units.

Working conditions changed for everyone in the wake of this new round of enlargement. The young 'Nordics' were not able to learn from their more long-established colleagues or rely on a strong pre-existing model, for the service had undergone radical changes. They were agents of change, particularly as regards computer technology, and sped up the changes in working methods. The translators in the new units typed their own texts, while the secretaries carried out administrative tasks. The profession of translator thus gradually evolved, keeping pace with the modernisation of the service.

It was at this point that French lost its status as the most widely used language within the Commission. The arrival of generations fluent mainly in that language accelerated the switch to English, something which had not happened in 1973. The increase from nine to 11 official languages and the arrival of Finnish, the first non-Indo-European language, marked the end of an era. There had been a time when translators were able to understand or even speak all the official languages of the Community, but this period was now over.

The translators of the new languages were familiar with the new technologies and adapted very quickly to the office

 **Find out more?**

*In Finland, the text of directly applicable legislation (regulations) is also authentic in Swedish by virtue of the country's bilingual system under its Constitution. Certain discrepancies emerged when the two versions became official in Finland, but it was not possible to determine whether they stemmed from the translation or from the English and French versions used for reference purposes.*

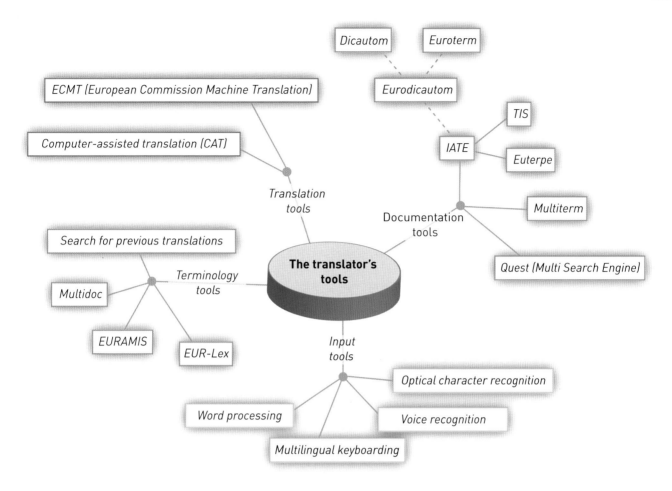

The translator's tools

technology and IT environment that was then emerging. Starting in the 1970s, the translation service had considered two *machine translation* systems, one based on conversion between pairs of language, the other combining grammar and multilingual corpuses of examples. The former system was selected for use and, at the start of the 1990s, a multilingual action plan was launched to use machine translation in certain areas (e.g. *anti-dumping* documents). Substantial language development work was carried out to encode into the systems the specialised terminology required and to import dictionaries.

In 1995, i.e. comparatively late, terminals were replaced by the first PCs, which were then introduced across the board over the next three years. They made it possible to incorporate word processing, office technology tools (particularly for document management) and translation aids, including in particular access to data banks such as

 **Find out more?**

*Further information on the tools available to translators is given at the end of this volume (p. 68).*

**Eur-Lex** (containing the Treaties, Community legislation and European case law) and **Eurodicautom** (the European Commission's terminology database), and a little later to Internet-based resources.

In 1998, the translation service made two innovations available to the Commission's departments: **SdTVista** and **Poetry** (software allowing the electronic transmission of documents for translation). It also introduced an application called **Suivi**, used to manage translation requests. A pilot phase of a computerised management program for external translations (Trèfle) started towards the end of the 1990s.

Technology thus provided the translator with new tools: systems for extracting complete texts, terminology systems, translation memories and machine translation.

These systems are now part and parcel of the European Commission translation service's workflow: **SdTVista** is used to search out complete texts from reference documents; **Euramis** creates translation memories which are stored in a central language resources database; for a small number of language combinations, sentences not found are automatically sent for machine translation; the relevant terminology is retrieved in batches from **Eurodicautom**.

The translator in this way receives the full benefit of terminological and documentation tools. They are essential for the service's productivity and for uniformity in documents. Whenever possible, material already translated is not re-translated. Thanks to these new technologies, particularly shared memories and search engines, the documentary and terminological infrastructure which existed hitherto has been considerably streamlined. A wide range of tools enables the translator to access not only concepts and definitions but also terms in context and in a variety of languages. The Internet enables translators to be more autonomous, particularly with regard to ad hoc research requirements. They are now at the hub of an array of integrated tools for local management and interactive processing of linguistic resources.

The tools at their disposal combine simultaneously machine translation, automatic retrieval of repetitive text, automatic alignment, **voice recognition**, consultation of a central translation memory, access to **Multiterm** and **Multidoc**, digitisation of non-electronic documents thanks to optical recognition software, etc.

This IT revolution had an impact on translators' working methods. The gradual transformation of the profession resulted in translators delivering a finished product, both from the linguistic standpoint and in terms of format. Electronic mail and electronic document management became the norm. In 1998, individual production stood at five pages per day and the number of pages translated yearly passed the million mark. It should be noted that 18% of this volume was produced by freelance translators. On the organisational side there was a change of culture: deadlines were negotiated by the planning department, access to huge memories was instantaneous, data sharing was systematic and any corrections barely perceptible. The paper trail was coming to an end. The Commission achieved a leap in quality which was unrivalled by the other European institutions.

In addition to the accession of three new Member States in 1995, European integration moved ahead slowly but surely. On 2 October 1997, the Amsterdam Treaty amending the Treaty establishing the European Community (EC Treaty) and the Treaty on European Union (Maastricht Treaty or EU Treaty) was signed by the 15 Member States. It came into force on 1 May 1999. The purpose was to create the political and institutional conditions needed to allow the European Union to rise to the challenges of the future with regard *inter alia* to rapid developments in the international situation, the globalisation of the economy and its repercussions on employment, the fight against terrorism, international crime and drug trafficking, ecological imbalances and threats to public health. This Treaty marked the first appearance in European legislation of the expression 'sustainable development'. The Maastricht Treaty had already mentioned this idea when it referred to 'cohesion and environmental protection', and the Amsterdam Treaty added the expression 'taking into account the principle of sustainable development'. It also introduced reinforced cooperation, i.e. the possibility for Member Sates that so wish to develop closer cooperation between themselves.

Meanwhile, the SdT was given a new Director-General. Edouard Brackeniers retired at the end of 1996, to be replaced by Colette Flesch. She remained at the helm until the end of 1997, the year of her election to the European Parliament. Brian McCluskey took over from her, and so for the very first time the translation service was led by a former translator.

In parallel with this, at the end of 1997 the Commission launched an internal evaluation exercise called DeCoDe (*Dessiner la Commission de demain –*

'Designing tomorrow's Commission'). The object of the exercise was to rationalise costs across the different Commission departments. This gave the translators an opportunity to explain their profession and to dispel the many misunderstandings concerning the immediate context of their work. According to the DPT, it was wrong to think that the ideal translator should have had both language and legal training. As Community documents spanned a huge range of subject areas (from agriculture to information technology, medicine, chemistry, economics, etc), it was clear for them that the idea of recruiting only lawyer-linguists was absurd inasmuch as the most diverse specialisations were invaluable to the task of translation.

In the wake of this work, the Commission adopted several strategic documents, particularly a decision on translation demand management, designed to strike the right balance between the maintenance of multilingualism and the deployment of optimum working methods.

At the beginning of 2000, the Translation Service drew up a multiannual programme to improve the integration of translation into the document production chain and to adapt staffing and organisation to future work. It highlighted the following problems: late changes to originals (equivalent to 20% of all the pages translated), excessively long documents and originals of poor quality. These considerations led the Commission – again with a view to rationalising resources – to propose, in December 2001, eleven measures aimed at standardising and simplifying language matters. It stressed the need on the one hand for stable, brief, high-quality originals drafted under the responsibility of the originating department and on the other for translation coordinated by the Translation Service. Since then, the Translation Service has also been able to give its opinion in the *"interservice consultation"* process just like any other department and thereby make linguistic improvements to originals, while undertaking to deliver, within 48 hours, the language versions required by the **College of Commissioners** for the adoption of an act. At the same time, the procedures for the adoption of acts by the College were simplified and a limit of twenty pages was introduced for documents to be submitted for adoption or approval. This restriction turned out to be very difficult to put into practice, however, and in 2009, the average length of a Commission Communication was 37 pages. Any documents for approval by the College by oral or written procedure could be submitted in the procedural languages without the other language versions, provided those other versions were not authentic or necessary for the act to enter into force. The various departments were encouraged to plan their requirements and to have their forecasts validated in agreement with a central programming unit of the Secretariat-General. In return, the Translation Service would be expected to ensure that the original and all language versions matched and to send documents direct to the Registry. This last decision could not be implemented until 2008. From being a simple service-provider, the Translation Service thus became a department with responsibilities in the policy-making and legislative processes.

The European Union's successes and the geopolitical changes in Europe after the fall of communism led to the idea of an eastward expansion of the EU. This project meant that the EU institutions needed to be reorganised to guarantee their smooth operation and appropriate measures needed to be adopted to ensure that the integration of Eastern Europe would be successful.

Therefore, following discussions and negotiations in the *intergovernmental conference* concluded in Nice at the end of 2000, on 26 February 2001 the Member States of the European Union signed a Treaty laying down the principles and methods for developing the institutional system as Europe expands. This was the Treaty of Nice, which came into force on 1 February 2003.

The prospect of enlargement to 27 Member States by 2007 meant that the decision-making procedures in the institutions needed to be revised. A new distribution of the votes allocated to each Member State in the Council and a new way of calculating the qualified majority were vital if that decision-making institution were not to grind to a halt. With the Treaty of Nice, the institutional reform needed for enlargement began, especially in the three main institutions of the European Union.

At first there was considerable uncertainty as to the number of countries to include. It was originally intended that only five countries would join in 2006, but in 2002 the Commission identified thirteen candidate countries and envisaged ten accessions. In the end, ten candidate countries were scheduled for accession in 2004.

The construction of Europe continued with the introduction, on 1 February 2002, of the euro, the successor to the **ECU** (European Currency Unit), as legal tender in twelve Member States of the Union.

The currency had been introduced at midnight on 1 January 1999: the national currencies of the participating countries – eleven at the time – had then ceased to exist in their own right and had become mere subdivisions of the European currency. The euro is the official currency of the European Union as a whole and the single currency used by the 16 of its Member States that form the euro area.

 **Find out more?**

*The euro area currently has 16 members, which joined on the following dates:*

*1/1/1999:  Germany, Austria, Belgium, Finland,
France, Ireland, Italy, Luxembourg,
Netherlands, Portugal;*
*1/1/2001:  Greece;*
*1/1/2007:  Slovenia;*
*1/1/2008:  Cyprus, Malta;*
*1/1/2009:  Slovakia.*

A new Director-General, Michel Vanden Abeele, was appointed in 2002. His mandate was to restructure the Translation Service in order to refocus its activities on the core business of the Commission, to increase productivity and to set up the translation capacities needed for the new languages resulting from the accession of ten new countries. The Translation Service (*SdT*) became the Directorate-General for Translation (**DGT**).

A major new reorganisation process was launched. The enlargement involving nine new languages, scheduled for 2004, made the operation of the service on the basis of a thematic structure hardly possible, since with twenty languages, a thematic structure would have required the creation of 120 units. The Director-General therefore decided to return to a linguistic structure. The compromise was to create thematic units within the monolingual language groups. Former thematic advisers became heads of language departments. This new structure was intended to facilitate consistency between the various units of a given language department and to provide a certain flexibility, in the form of the possibility of transferring documents between different thematic units in the event of an excessive workload. The grouping by language also promoted the cohesion of the new teams of translators. On the downside, however, this new structure tended to reduce the flow of multilingual and multinational exchanges.

In parallel, DGT continued to reflect on the future of translation within the institution. This led, in 2002, to the Commission's adopting a Communication extending the measures taken at the end of 2001. DGT defined its "core task" – the translation of documents relating to the essential functions of the institution (legislation and texts that are confidential or connected with the autonomy of the institution) – with a view to optimising the management of demand. A system of categorising documents was established, as a basis for negotiations with requesters. It was also planned to increase the proportion of freelanced work from 20% to 30%, with DGT nevertheless continuing to bear full responsibility.

DGT quickly mobilised in preparation for the enlargement to Eastern Europe, with action on a number of fronts: training of translators in the new languages, advice to the units coordinating translation work in the new countries, exploring the local market for external translators, contacts with local centres for training translators, and organising visits to DGT for officials from candidate countries responsible for the translation of EU legislation. A *Task Force* was set up in 2000 to coordinate administrative and budgetary preparations, interinstitutional cooperation, revision of secondary legislation, selection of translators and assistants, and the adaptation of aids to translation.

The service may well have successfully managed the 1995 enlargement, but the 2004 exercise was unprecedented. The number and the historical and linguistic variety of the countries (countries of Central Europe, the former USSR and the former Yugoslavia, together with islands in the Mediterranean) made preparations for membership more complex. Moreover, the EU had decided to conduct this enlargement as quickly as possible, which meant very tight turnaround times for the translation and revision of the existing body of Community legislation. It was also decided that all the new languages should have equal status to the existing ones right from the date of accession. This decision meant major risks for the translation service, particularly as regards competitions and staff-recruitment procedures.

This expansion therefore coincided with a major reorganisation of DGT, while its management also went through a period of instability. After the departure of Michel Vanden Abeele in mid-2003, Fernand Thurmes was Acting Director-General until the arrival in early 2004 of a new Director-General, Karl-Johan Lönnroth. The disturbing situation confronting the service at the time meant that the new Director-General had to find innovative and radical solutions very quickly. The years 2003 to 2005 were years of crisis management.

DGT worked on preparing for enlargement in close cooperation with DG Enlargement (TAIEX), which is responsible for the accession of new members to the European Union. The candidate countries each set up a unit to coordinate translation – usually incorporated into the Ministry of Justice or the Ministry of Foreign Affairs. These units were responsible for translating all **Community law** into the respective national languages and revising it. The translation and revision of the **acquis communautaire** was thus done locally. The legal services of the three institutions finalised and certified the translations into the nine new languages before they were published in a special edition of the Official Journal. TAIEX organised the translation into English and French of parts of national legislation of which the compliance with Community law needed to be verified. DGT was successful in ensuring that the translations were done with tools compatible with its own, so that the Community legislation could be retrieved for subsequent work following the signing of the accession Treaties, since, in the absence of a derogation, DGT was obliged, as from the date of accession, to provide full language cover and to translate the Commission's legislative initiatives into all the official languages.

With the doubling of the number of official languages it was feared that the Commission's translation budget would increase by almost 80%. One solution was to increase the proportion of freelance translations from 20% to 40%. In the face of this threat to the budget, some officials of the European Commission thought that **machine translation** might help solve the problem. Admittedly, machine translation had proved useful for fast translation of letters from members

The 2004 Enlargement

of the public and for texts of minimal importance, but since the quality was poor, it was totally unusable for translating legislation. Moreover, it was not available in any of the "new" languages. This option was quickly rejected, therefore.

DGT used various methods for building up the translation capacities that would be needed after accession. It first compiled, through a call for expressions of interest, a file of approved external translators for all the new languages. In March 2003 it launched, together with the other European institutions, a joint invitation to tender focusing on the new languages, alongside its own general invitation to tender aimed at meeting the needs in all the official languages, both existing and new.

In connection with the enlargement of the EU from 15 to 25 members, a European Personnel Selection Office (**EPSO**) was set up, and it was responsible for organising competitions open to nationals of the new Member States. DGT worked in close cooperation with EPSO, the Enlargement DG and the

Personnel and Administration DG to recruit competent staff, and also to develop the IT infrastructure, office accommodation and social facilities needed for the new staff.

Since the lists of successful applicants were insufficient to fill the permanent posts, temporary staff had to be recruited and would be assigned to Luxembourg. It was decided to base the translators of the languages of the ten new Member States in the Grand Duchy in order to respect the agreements concluded at intergovernmental level on the seats of the institutions. The result is that about half of DGT staff are based in Luxembourg. The European quarter in Luxembourg took on a new lease of life with the arrival of lots of young officials, many of them women, together with their families, which led in particular to the need to increase the capacity of the schools to accommodate their children.

In October 2003, 45 new members of staff were recruited, and by spring 2004 DGT had 10% of the resources it needed, taking all languages together. It had to repeat the procedure in 2004 and 2005, however, to achieve the target figures, especially as the translation market is very small in some countries such as Malta, Slovenia and the Baltic States.

The budgetary authority (i.e. the Council and the European Parliament) initially granted DGT posts a third at a time over three years (2004 to 2006). Despite this restriction, the new language units, comprising a dozen translators each at the beginning of 2004, were immediately required to cope with a full normal work pattern. Moreover, the candidate countries had not managed to translate the entire body of Community legislation into the nine new languages in time. Temporary staff were therefore recruited as reinforcements.

The new Director-General, Karl-Johan Lönnroth, was appointed head of DGT in January 2004. At that time the service was in a critical situation and a quick recovery was needed. The DGT budget had been increased by only 30%, whereas the number of official languages had doubled. The problem of demand management took on unprecedented proportions. The Director-General got down to work immediately, therefore, and submitted several proposals to the Commission for remedying the situation. On May 26 2004, following a proposal by DGT, the Commission adopted a communication regulating the use of translation under three headings. First of all demand needed to be managed: fewer documents should be translated and they must be shorter. Temporary staff then had to be recruited to establish an operational workforce as quickly as possible. Finally, the need to plan the workflow was highlighted. This last point meant that DGT should be involved in the process of preparing Commission documents, particularly as regards the strategic planning work by the Secretariat General. It was also decided to reduce the length of documents intended for the College of Commissioners to not more than fifteen pages.

The impact of this decision was considerable for both the institution and DGT. The growth in demand that the service was faced with before 2004 because of the introduction of the euro, the implementation of the Treaty of Amsterdam and the preparations for enlargement, which had been accompanied by a drop in staff numbers, came to an end. The workload fell by 30% for the eleven old languages. However, unlike on the occasion of the previous enlargement in 1995, there were no exceptions for the new languages, apart from Maltese. This resulted in considerable overwork for the new language departments because of a shortage of human resources.

The demand-management strategy caused a disturbance throughout the institution because of the restrictions imposed. Furthermore, some Member States complained about no longer having certain categories of document in their language. There were initial protests from certain quarters, including the Directorates-General responsible for new policies such as Justice and Home Affairs (**JHA**) or those that introduce legislative packages in waves (such as **TREN**, **ENV** and **INFSO**) but after a short period of shock during the summer of 2004 the various departments adapted to the new rules. Some also welcomed the fact that the Commission's messages had become more clear-cut and better targeted. Officials responsible for drafting learnt to separate out the non-legislative parts of documents and to submit them as working documents – a category that is given only partial linguistic treatment (one to three languages at the most). They also changed the way they wrote and texts became more concise. The profile of translations also changed considerably. The work was refocused on documents that were considered essential, i.e. legislation (one quarter of the workload in 2003 and more than one third in 2005) and policy documents.

This demand management marked a break with the previous period. Henceforth, the procedural-language departments (German, English and French) would be required to keep pace with the work of the College of Commissioners. They also continued to translate other working documents which had to be made available only in a limited number of languages. These departments translated an increasing proportion of English originals into French and German.

The introduction of the new translation strategy gradually increased the gap between the procedural-language departments and the other language departments, with the latter seeing a substantial reduction in their workload, since the volume of studies or research projects, very long or very technical documents, and committee working documents or invitations to tender, which had been translated internally over the 1970s and 1980s, fell relative to key documents, such as legislation.

After the upheavals caused by the 2004 enlargement, the EU decided to accept two new countries in 2007: Bulgaria and Romania. The preparation for the accession of these two countries was a success story. Thanks to the changes introduced in 2004 and the establishment of demand management, DGT had learnt a number of lessons that enabled it to have the administrative stability it needed – in terms of recruitment and integration of human resources, translation of the existing body of Community legislation, availability of contractors and external linguistic and terminological support – in order to embark on a medium- and long-term strategy. In March 2006, the service was reorganised in order to synchronise the work of all the language departments (including the new languages), which, with the exception of French and German, were henceforth each divided into only three units. DGT in Brussels moved to a new site, which was more up-to-date and able to accommodate the entire staff.

By 1 February 2007, particularly thanks to the support of the TAIEX office, translation of the pre-accession acquis had been 79% completed on average for the two countries (the figure had been only 72% for the ten accession countries on 1 June 2004, with considerable variation between countries). The accession of the two countries and the integration of officials speaking the new languages therefore went off smoothly.

The DGT has undergone several major changes during its history, but structural changes have only slightly affected the immediate working environment of translators. Commission translators work with three type of text: incoming, outgoing and internal documents. The documents to be translated into all 23 languages are essentially the language versions to be published in the Official Journal, translated from originals written mostly in English. It follows that nowadays the English-language department operates differently from the other departments, since it is the only department that receives incoming documents in all the official languages (and often other languages too), such as periodic reports, Member States' national legislation, letters from national and regional administrations, State aid dossiers, documents concerning infringements of the Treaties and formal complaints to the Commission.

In addition, DGT now produces two types of document. On the one hand there is the traditional production of legislation, using specific Community terminology, in 23 equivalent language versions, while on the other hand there are communication documents addressed directly to citizens in the Member States, which are more geared to the different national cultures and are aimed at localising the message for the respective target groups. These are texts published on the internet or press releases aimed at transposing the Community policies concerned into the administrative language and culture of a given country.

Recently, to cope with the influx of documents from the Member States of Central Europe, DGT has introduced, on an experimental and voluntary basis, the possibility for translators to do **two-way translation**, i.e. to work also into a language other than their mother tongue. The documents concerned by this option are newspaper articles or letters from individuals, companies, pressure groups, local, regional or national authorities and various stakeholders written in their native languages. In most cases, the translations are revised by a native speaker.

These major changes have necessitated a new organisation chart. Alongside the translation Directorates, a "Translation Strategy" Directorate has come into being, with the task of implementing demand-management policy and the outsourcing, evaluation and analysis policies. It also provides support functions, such as coordination of terminology and the policy of multilingualism. The Central Planning Unit, which previously reported directly to the Director-General, has been incorporated into this new Directorate. Three units now come directly under the Director-General: Legal, Interinstitutional and National Affairs, Audit, and Communication and Information.

Today, DGT is a service that responds to the policy priorities of the Commission. Since 2006, this new status has led to several changes in the structure of the service with a view to improving the quality of texts in the **source languages**, reinforcing the local European information points and providing multilingual information for the people of Europe on major EU policies and the Commission's priorities.

Communication with the public has become a major priority in the European Union, especially since the negative outcomes of the referenda on the Constitutional Treaty in the Netherlands and France in April and May 2005.

The Commission has therefore adopted a series of initiatives designed to improve the quality of communication. The information available on the Internet is now localised, as this is crucial for the public's proper understanding of the European Union and essential to support the process of ratifying EU Treaties.

The translation and adaptation of the content of the website of the EU institutions ("Europa") are carried out by a multilingual unit of translators specialising in communication on the Internet. This unit is made up of 23 language groups, with four or five translators per language, and has taken over this work from the language departments. The style of translation is geared to

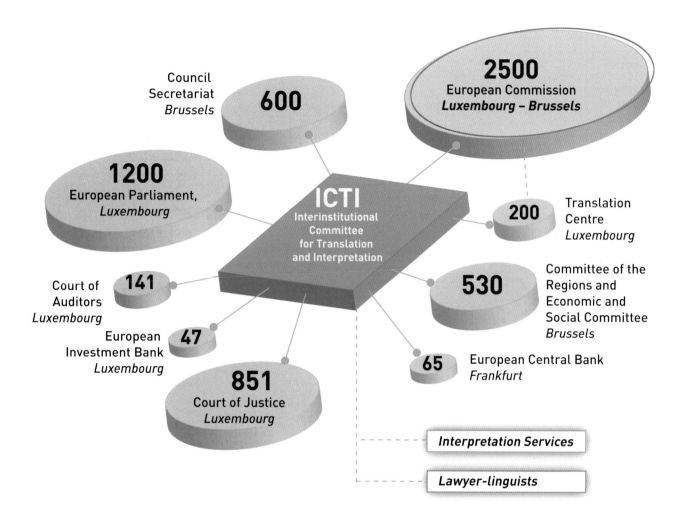

Interinstitutional cooperation on translation and interpretation

 **Find out more?**

The ICTI was set up in 1995 at the initiative of the heads of the various bodies and brings together representatives of all the translation and interpretation services of the European institutions and other bodies.

Since its inception, the committee has been coordinating and implementing interinstitutional projects and

managing IATE. Each year the ICTI submits a report to the EU institutions reviewing the progress in interinstitutional cooperation in the field of translation and interpretation and suggesting avenues for taking this further.

For 2009 and 2010, the Chair of the Committee is held by the Commission in the person of its Director-General of Translation, Karl-Johan Lönnroth.

the Internet: the message is more condensed, and a simple style promotes efficiency. The aim must be to find the word that will catch people's attention and appear in an Internet search.

With its "Web" unit, translation has taken up the challenge of the instant, interactive and ephemeral communication that is characteristic of exchanges on the Internet. This means that translators must be able to handle cultural conventions and adapt their communication strategy. Meanwhile, the transition to the information society is continuing. Future generations will know only a computerised world, where the information sent out is increasingly concise and for immediate consumption. This is another challenge for DGT, which must adapt to these changes and be ever more innovative to meet future challenges.

DGT is also active in interinstitutional cooperation in the field of translation. It is a member of the Interinstitutional Committee for Translation and Interpretation (ICTI), an organisation in which the language services of the institutions and bodies of the European Union cooperate.

DGT has also diversified the services and training it offers. One of the things on offer is a linguistic revision service for authors in the various Directorates-General writing in a language other than their mother tongue. Considering that at least 80% of original documents are now written in English, improving the language quality has become a priority and DGT has responded to this by setting up, in 2006, a unit providing linguistic and stylistic revision of English and French originals. This service for authors should also help simplify the work of translation into 23 languages.

In order to improve training for the profession of translator, DGT is working on a European Master's in Translation (EMT) project to be launched in several universities across Europe. The project aims at providing high-quality training for students holding a first degree in languages or another subject of relevance to the requirements of translation in the EU institutions (terminological work, information technology as an aid to translation, specialist fields and their languages, intercultural communication etc.). Students will also learn to adapt to market constraints and will be trained to meet new translation requirements (audiovisual, subtitles, etc.).

 **Find out more?**

*E-learning involves teaching via a computer alternating with a teacher in a classroom.*

The training on offer for Commission translators has also evolved since the inception of the Communities, and is now included when calculating the cost of good translation. It is essential for the quality of translations. All Community officials are encouraged throughout their career to follow training courses to improve their language, IT or other specific skills. Officials in general, however, are confronted less than translators with the need to expand and constantly update their skills, especially as regards language learning or the acquisition of knowledge in an extremely wide range of fields. Nowadays, therefore, the training on offer is tailored to the needs of translators. The courses for learning a language are currently spread over four years, spanning eight levels (including two advanced, which are mandatory for translators).

Some courses (particularly Maltese) are provided in the form of *e-learning*, which has also been introduced for **conversion courses** between twin languages (such as Czech and Slovak). Translators also receive general training offered by other Commission departments, such as the Ariane series of courses, which presents the interinstitutional legislative and decision-making procedures. DGT is currently launching a skills inventory to identify training needs throughout all the departments in connection with the major issues in the Commission's programme, since to translate correctly, one must understand the reality behind the words. Good translation means grasping not only the ramifications but also the background.

Over the past decade, the role of DGT has become increasingly geared to policy, and in 2008 there was therefore a minor reorganisation aimed at creating synergies. Terminological coordination and the library were merged into a single unit, the European Master's in Translation programme was attached to the multilingualism sector, and computer support was partly transferred to the Informatics DG (DIGIT).

The desire to rationalise internal operations and costs led to the adoption of a new policy: *"Total Quality Management"*.

The considerable efforts made by the service and the streamlining of its operations have enabled DGT to meet the Commission's ongoing and new requirements in a European Union operating in 23 languages, which has brought the number of possible language combinations up to 506 .

Enlargement and the integration of the new countries into the functioning of the European Union have been among the institution's prim, and the Commission created a portfolio focused on multilingualism policy, since the language dimension had become more than ever before a sign of integration, of respect for citizens and of what makes Europe different. The policy of multilingualism needs to be conducted in an efficient and balanced fashion so that the new European Union can function properly and gear itself to the future.

**Find out more?**

*"Total Quality Management" is a DGT policy that defines 22 actions to be carried out in 2009 to provide solutions – particularly as regards the need for feedback from customers, the perceived ignorance of the nature and destination of documents, lack of thematic expertise etc.*

# Multilingualism: the birth of a fully-fledged policy

THERE HAVE BEEN significant changes, therefore, with a view to making DGT much more efficient, integrating it into the Commission's decision-making process and providing it with a strategy based on an analysis of the requirements associated with multilingualism. DGT now plays a genuinely active role in policy-making and also contributes to the policy of multilingualism established by the Commission on 22 November 2005.

In order to support the legitimacy, effectiveness and transparency of the European Union and its wish to serve the people of Europe, DGT provides the European Commission with language services of a high quality for its written communications in all the official languages, thus promoting multilingualism in the European Union.

The ultimate goal of the European Union is set out in Article 1 of the Treaty on European Union (TEU): "creating an ever closer union among the peoples of Europe, in which decisions are taken as openly as possible and as closely as possible to the citizen". A clause in this Treaty also stipulates that the Union must respect "the national identities of its Member States." Multilingualism is therefore one of the fundamental principles of the European Union, because it means that all the official languages are equal in law.

Equal status for the official languages goes right to the heart of what Europe is about, since language is an important part of both national and personal identity. We all see ourselves through the medium of the language we speak from birth. It is therefore essential to give equal status to all EU languages so that everyone feels respected and included as a European citizen.

All European legislation is, in one way or another, binding on those to whom it is addressed and must therefore be translated. Respect for democracy depends on these translations. It is a legal requirement and a democratic necessity to present Community legislation to European citizens in their mother tongues to ensure their equality before the law. Ignorance of the law is no excuse, which is why the law cannot be imposed in a foreign language that people cannot understand. Citizens can access Community law through the *Official Journal of the European Union*, in which many of the translations produced by DGT are published. It is published each working day in all the official languages of the European Union.

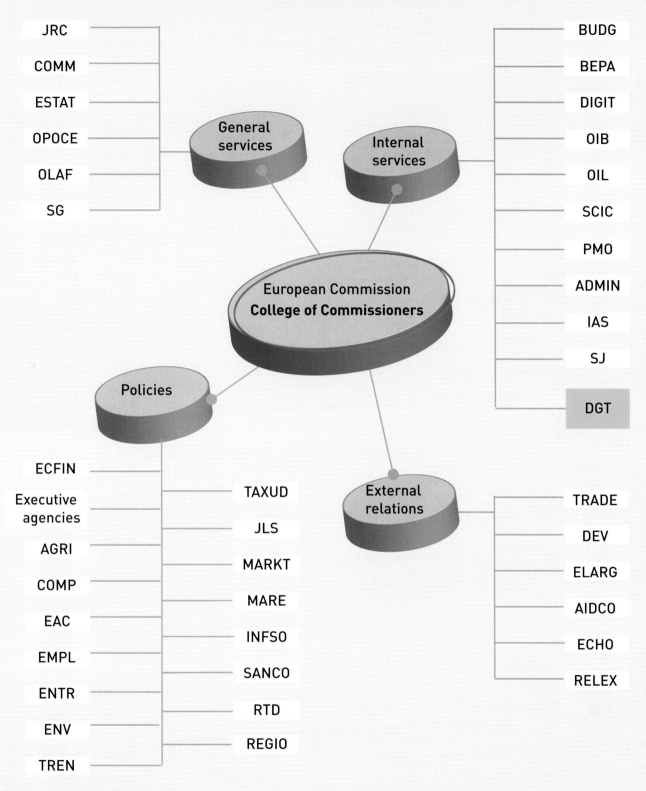

Structure of the European Commission, 2009

*(Full names of the European Commission departments are given at the end of the volume.)*

Translation turns out to be an essential element in each of many stages of producing legislation. It is fundamental in the preparation of working documents (which often include a substantial amount of technical documentation), in the discussion of draft versions (which calls for an extensive consultation process) and in the formulation of the final text, since that represents a commitment by the Commission and must by its nature reach a wide range of readers. Finally, translation is needed in the preparation of the written information that the Commission is required to circulate at all levels once a proposal has been adopted and during the discussion and amendment of proposals in the European Parliament and the Council before finalisation.

Article 255 of the Treaty of Amsterdam introduced the right of access for all European citizens to European Parliament, Council and Commission documents, which has obvious implications for translation. In this context, the translation of Community law becomes even more essential for respecting democracy, as access to legal documents means that versions must be produced in a language that citizens can understand.

Over the last fifty years, the number of official languages has increased gradually from four to twenty-three. When a new Member State joins the European Union, the Treaties are translated into the language of the country in question and this new language version is deemed "authentic" (that is to say, it has legal force) in the same way as the four original versions. Thus, the founding Treaties of the European Union now exist in 23 languages.

It is important to note that there are no versions of Treaties in the various regional languages, since the "official languages" of the Member States are those indicated by the States in question during the accession negotiations.

The choice is not dictated by the European institutions. It is the Member States themselves who decide. Each time an enlargement is in prospect, each candidate countries presents in the course of the negotiations its wishes concerning the language or languages to be used in contacts between that country (or its citizens) and the institutions. It is then the Member Sates as a whole who decide unanimously to amend Regulation No 1 and add another language to the official languages of the European Union.

 **Find out more?**

*The official languages selected by a Member State in the negotiations for accession to the European Union must be the official language or one or the official languages of that State under its Constitution.*

This is why the 27 Member States of the European Union have only 23 official languages: some of them share one or more official languages with another Member State (Austria, Germany and Luxembourg share German, Ireland, the United Kingdom and Malta share English etc.).

Although multilingualism is a key element in the construction of Europe – a pillar of its democracy – there is no legal basis for it, since the Treaty of Paris (which established the ECSC in 1951) does not mention multilingualism. In fact, this first Treaty was authentic only in French. Nor was the problem of languages or a policy of multilingualism mentioned in the two Treaties of Rome signed in 1957. Thus, when the two Treaties of Rome entered into force on 1 January 1958, the first Regulation adopted by the Council of Ministers concerned the official languages and the **working languages** to be used. This was Regulation No 1 of 1958, which is, in a sense, the language charter of the Union. The official languages are listed in Article 1, and Article 5 stipulates that the *Official Journal* must be published in all these languages. Article 4 of this Regulation requires that texts be drafted in 23 languages – the term "draft" is used to avoid speaking of "translation". Officially, therefore, texts published in all the official languages do not exist in one original version with 22 translations, but in 23 language versions or even 23 originals.

Translation is mentioned nowhere in the legislation. This is the logical consequence of the principle that all languages have equal status. The concept of multiple authenticity safeguards equal rights for all languages and, by extension, the national identities of the Member States. This reflects the desire not to have any dominant language or culture in the European Union.

Over time, multilingualism has become a priority for the European Union. Since the 2004 enlargement, its significance has been such that the European Commission has decided to pursue an intensive, proactive policy focused exclusively on languages, cultural diversity and the promotion of multilingualism, in order to preserve what is different about Europe. The policy of multilingualism was instituted by the first Barroso Commission in 2005. Jan Figel' was the first Commissioner for multilingualism, and the first communication on multilingualism was published in November 2005. Initially, the policy of multilingualism was part of a portfolio with other policies, but subsequently, in 2007, the growing importance of the language question within the European Union led to the creation of a portfolio devoted exclusively to the policy of multilingualism, for which a separate Commissioner, Leonard Orban, was responsible until the end of 2009.

Multilingualism suffers in Europe from a number of misconceptions. Several myths die hard. The first, and the most widespread, is that all documents of the European Union are translated into all the languages. This is not the case. Only legislation and various outgoing documents are translated into all the official languages, as they are of general application and have to be published. For incoming documents, on the other hand, it may be sufficient to translate them into only one language, for information.

The second myth is that a huge proportion of the budget of the European Union is spent on multilingualism, whereas the costs of translation and interpretation in all the EU institutions account for less than 1% of the total annual budget of the European Union (corresponding to approximately €2 per head of population). At the Commission, the annual costs for translation are estimated at €300 million – which is equivalent to about €0.60 per head of population per year and a modest price to pay for guaranteeing democracy and equal rights among citizens.

Finally, the last of the most widespread myths is that it would be easy to reduce the number of working languages. Of course, superfluous translation and interpretation can often be avoided, but it is nevertheless vital not to underestimate the political importance of multilingualism and the difficulty of altering the language system. Therefore, all proposals for reductions in the number of languages have been rejected not only by the Member States but also for legal reasons. The same also applies to attempts to introduce a formal distinction between *"official languages"* (for legislation etc.) and *"working languages"* (for internal use at meetings, etc.). Currently, there is no formal distinction between the two. In the Commission, the term *"procedural languages"* is used to refer to English, French and German, as these are the languages in which documents must be produced for the work of the College of Commissioners. The other twenty *"non-procedural"* language versions still have to be produced, but for a later date, usually 48 hours after the meeting.

However, even though it is used for practical reasons of internal functioning, the concept of "procedural language" has no basis in law; it relates exclusively to the internal workings of the Commission, since when representatives of the

Member States discuss the legislative proposals of the European Union, they expect to have all the language versions, and if they did not that could cause political incidents.

Because of these considerations and facts, multilingualism has become one of the liveliest policy areas of the European Union, with DGT currently playing a major role in publicising and promoting this policy. It works together with other DGs (EAC, SCIC, PO etc.) on drafting the Commissioner for Multilingualism's speeches, organises events to promote languages (conferences, competitions, studies) and so on.

The new structure and new geopolitical realities have meant that DGT has acquired the status of a Directorate-General with a role in European policy-making, in which it is now an essential element as the representative of languages and the guarantor of multilingualism in the European Union.

The European Union also needs to be brought up to date so that it can respond to current and future realities in a globalised world, since although the EU has greatly expanded since 2004, its institutions still operate in the same was as they did at the outset. The decision-making process may well have been suitable for a Europe of 6 or 15, but in a Europe of 27 it needs to be revamped to ensure its smooth running.

These considerations are the subject of the Treaty signed in Lisbon on December 13 2007. Political, economic and social developments led the Heads of State and of Government to agree on new rules to govern future action by the Union. The objective of the Lisbon Treaty is to adapt the European institutions and their working methods to new circumstances, to strengthen the democratic legitimacy of the Union, and to consolidate the foundation of core values.

For DGT and for the multilingualism portfolio, the entry into force of the Lisbon Treaty in December 2009 presents a number of challenges but also affords new prospects. Changes are needed in terms of both policy and operation. The main challenges will derive from the rules laid down in the "new *comitology*" Regulation and the general principles concerning mechanisms for scrutinising the exercise of implementing powers by the Commission. The workflow will also be modified by the creation of new categories of acts and the consultation of national parliaments, which has become compulsory under the Treaty. The application of the codecision procedure is also to be extended, which will generate additional translation requests. The potential impact on translation of citizens' initiatives also needs to be assessed. Finally, special attention must be given to the procedures for setting up the European External-Action Service to ensure that the Commission retains its full powers of initiative and prerogatives, even on matters relating to translation, while the necessary resources and the relevant mechanisms are being put in place.

DGT will thus face several major challenges in the coming years. Its role as a pillar of the multilingualism policy and its vital efforts to respect equality between the citizens of Europe will place the service at the heart of the deployment of European policies.

For half a century, thousands of linguists have worked to create new communication channels, to provide access to European ideas for a growing number of citizens, and to make European integration a successful and democratic process. The road travelled since the 1950s, when translation was merely a service, until today, when it has become a policy factor of the first order, has been long and laborious. DGT is ready to continue along this path in the future and to take up the challenges that lie ahead.

# In conclusion ...

If the people of Europe consider that they are understood, accepted and respected in their own culture, they will feel like citizens of Europe. Language lies at the heart of what makes people individuals – hence respect for the diversity of language is crucial to respect for the individual. In Europe, multilingualism has a key role to play in underpinning democracy and citizens' rights and its future is assured within a European Union which is destined to grow and to embrace new peoples and new languages. In the years to come there will be ever-increasing contact between languages, both within Europe and throughout the wider world. Multilingual exchanges will lead to greater integration amongst peoples who will feel that their cultural identity has been acknowledged, thanks to the efforts made to address them in their native tongue.

Multilingualism is also a challenge for Europe and for its citizens. Major efforts will clearly have to be made with regard to education systems and to communication with a general public of ever-increasing cultural and linguistic diversity, in order to make the European Union an exemplary alliance capable of serving as a reference. Multilingualism is a challenge for the European institutions as well; the Commission has managed to constantly adapt to the requirements stemming from its language rules whilst ensuring that the Community machine continues to run smoothly, and it will undoubtedly respond superbly to the challenges which lie ahead.

The ubiquity of multilingualism will require much more frequent use to be made of translators and interpreters, since no one will be able to master all of the European Union's languages. Links of various kinds will therefore have to be built in order to enable people to understand one another, live together and experience one another's cultures. Translation will continue to be a bridge between nations, a key to understanding other peoples and the factor which increasingly humanises the European Union. In the words of Umberto Eco, translation will be 'the language of Europe'.

# The Directorate-General for Translation in 2009

DGT global staff figures*
Situation on 1 January 2010
(officials and temporary
agents)

Management 100
Field Offices 33
Translators 1413
Brussels 1144
Men 799
AST 544
Women 1537
Other AD 147
Field Offices 33
Web translators 99
Luxembourg 1159

| Nationalities in DGT | | |
|---|---|---|
| Belgian | BEL | 229 |
| Bulgarian | BGR | 73 |
| Czech | CZE | 73 |
| Danish | DNK | 86 |
| German | DEU | 165 |
| Estonian | EST | 74 |
| Irish | IRL | 28 |
| Greek | GRC | 134 |
| Spanish | ESP | 129 |
| French | FRA | 108 |
| Italian | ITA | 144 |
| Cypriot | CYP | 0 |
| Latvian | LVA | 69 |
| Lithuanian | LTU | 74 |
| Luxembourgish | LUX | 13 |
| Hungarian | HUN | 75 |
| Maltese | MLT | 62 |
| Dutch | NLD | 47 |
| Austrian | AUT | 10 |
| Polish | POL | 81 |
| Portuguese | PRT | 112 |
| Romanian | RON | 82 |
| Slovenian | SVN | 72 |
| Slovak | SVK | 70 |
| Finnish | FIN | 108 |
| Swedish | SWE | 83 |
| British | GBR | 135 |
| Total | | 2336 |

| Function groups in DGT | Total |
|---|---|
| Senior Managers | 6 |
| Middle Managers | 94 |
| Translators | 1413 |
| Web translators | 99 |
| Field Offices | 33 |
| Administrators | 147 |
| Assistants | 544 |
| Total | 2336 |

| Place of employment | |
|---|---|
| Field Offices | 33 |
| Brussels | 1144 |
| Luxembourg | 1159 |
| Total | 2336 |

| Gender | |
|---|---|
| Men | 799 |
| Women | 1537 |
| Total | 2336 |

* Source: Directorate-General for Translation - 01.01.2010.

## Target language in %   Pages translated in total

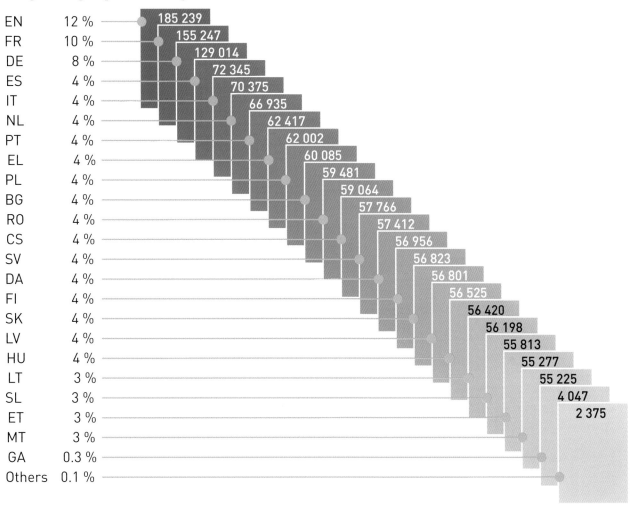

| | | |
|---|---|---|
| EN | 12 % | 185 239 |
| FR | 10 % | 155 247 |
| DE | 8 % | 129 014 |
| ES | 4 % | 72 345 |
| IT | 4 % | 70 375 |
| NL | 4 % | 66 935 |
| PT | 4 % | 62 417 |
| EL | 4 % | 62 002 |
| PL | 4 % | 60 085 |
| BG | 4 % | 59 481 |
| RO | 4 % | 59 064 |
| CS | 4 % | 57 766 |
| SV | 4 % | 57 412 |
| DA | 4 % | 56 956 |
| FI | 4 % | 56 823 |
| SK | 4 % | 56 801 |
| LV | 4 % | 56 525 |
| HU | 4 % | 56 420 |
| LT | 3 % | 56 198 |
| SL | 3 % | 55 813 |
| ET | 3 % | 55 277 |
| MT | 3 % | 55 225 |
| GA | 0.3 % | 4 047 |
| Others | 0.1 % | 2 375 |

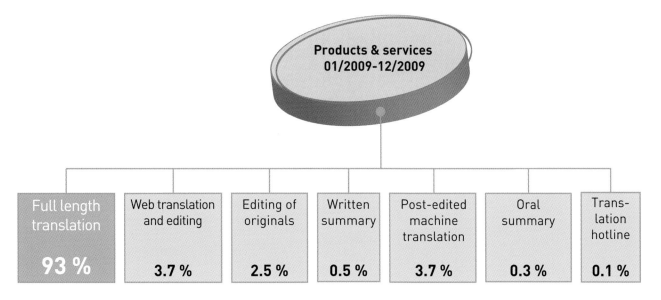

### Products & services
### 01/2009-12/2009

| Full length translation | Web translation and editing | Editing of originals | Written summary | Post-edited machine translation | Oral summary | Trans-lation hotline |
|---|---|---|---|---|---|---|
| **93 %** | **3.7 %** | **2.5 %** | **0.5 %** | **3.7 %** | **0.3 %** | **0.1 %** |

# Structure of the Directorate-General for Translation in 2009

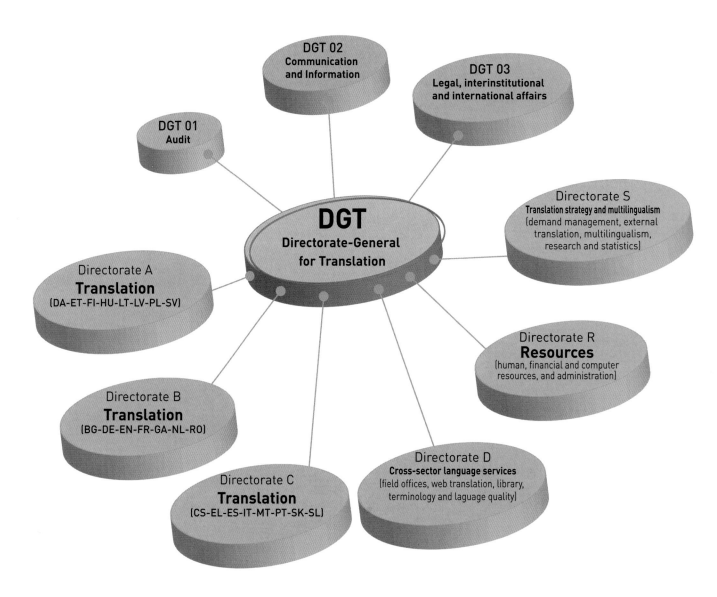

# Number of translators (1958-2009)

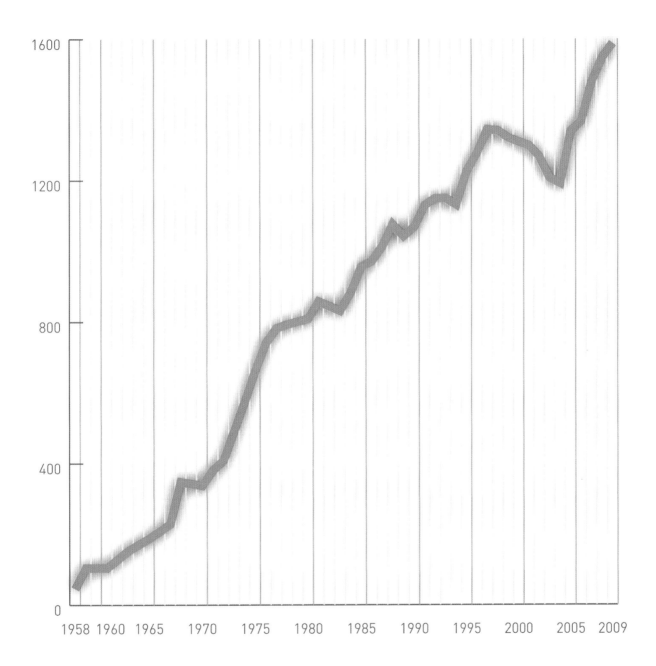

# Commission Presidents

| | Name | Post held from | Post held until |
|---|---|---|---|
| | Walter Hallstein | 10 January 1958 | 6 July 1967 |
| | Jean Rey | 7 July 1967 | 30 June 1970 |
| | Franco Maria Malfatti | 1 July 1970 | 21 March 1972 |
| | Sicco Leendert Mansholt | 22 March 1972 | 5 January 1973 |
| | François-Xavier Ortoli | 6 January 1973 | 5 January 1977 |
| | Roy Jenkins | 6 January 1977 | 5 January 1981 |
| | Gaston Thorn | 6 January 1981 | 5 January 1985 |
| | Jacques Delors | 6 January 1985 | 22 January 1995 |
| | Jacques Santer | 23 January 1995 | 15 March 1999 |
| | Manuel Marín | 16 March 1999 | 15 September 1999 |
| | Romano Prodi | 16 September 1999 | 21 November 2004 |
| | José Manuel Durão Barroso | 22 November 2004 | current President |

# Directors-General for Translation

Edouard Brackeniers

1990–1996

Colette Flesch

1997–1999

Brian McCluskey

1999–2002

Michel
Vanden Abeele

2002–2003

Karl-Johan (Juhani)
Lönnroth

2004–

*Current
Director-General*

# Overview of translation tool

| Tool | Background and characteristics |
|------|--------------------------------|
| Computer-assisted translation (TWB) | TWB (Translator's Workbench) is a software application produced by the Trados company which allows data obtained through the alignment of two language versions of a given document to be handled locally and processed interactively, through consultation of a central translation memory, for the translation of a new document. It was adopted by the Commission's translation service following a call for tenders. |
| DGTVista (remplacing SdTVista) | System in use since 1994 for the electronic filing of originals and translations (3.7 million documents in 23 languages) and equipped with a fast search engine. |
| Dicautom | Computerised dictionary developed in the 1960s, the glossaries of which were all in phraseological form. |
| Euramis (European Advanced Multilingual Information System) | The Euramis system is a platform combining terminology databases, computer-assisted translation and automatic translation. Euramis enables IATE to be consulted automatically from within a text, with the result of the search displayed in Multiterm format. It also enables equivalences or near-equivalences to be searched for phraseologically. Through automatic consultation of the language-resource database developed in connection with Euramis, phrases equivalent or approximating to those contained in the document to be translated can be found on a server. Euramis also enables all the legislative instruments referred to in the document to be retrieved from Eur-Lex, in both the source and the target language. Euramis currently (as at 30 November 2009) contains 72 599 772 source segments (i.e. phrases from original documents to be translated) and 258 291 337 target segments (i.e. translated segments), i.e. a total of 330 891 109 segments. |
| Eur-Lex (the replacement for CELEX) | A database comprising mainly European treaties, legislation and case-law. |
| Eurodicautom | Eurodicautom was the result of the 1967 merger of Euroterm and Dicautom. It was a computerised database initially fed via terminals and subsequently transferred to computers. Eurodicautom was the most important of the Community institutions' terminology databases, offering entries in all the European Union's official languages and in Latin. In 1995 it was decided that Eurodicautom would be merged with other institutions' terminology databases (see IATE). |
| Euroterm | Euroterm was the result of the electronic trawling of all multilingual texts created through the operation of the common market, as carried out in 1964 by the EEC. |
| IATE (Inter-Agency Terminology Exchange) | Eurodicautom (a Commission database), TIS (Terminology Information System – the Council's database) and Euterpe (the Parliament's database) were merged into IATE in 2002. IATE became publicly accessible in 2007. |

| Tool | Background and characteristics |
|---|---|
| Machine translation (ECMT – European Commission Machine Translation) | Machine translation was introduced at the Commission as early as 1976 and became more widely used once it became accessible via e-mail. It is currently available in 16 language combinations (of which eight give satisfactory results). Machine translation may enable the recipient of a text to form a general idea of the content if he or she has no knowledge of the source language, and hence to decide whether a proper translation is called for. It must be used to translate solely into a user's mother tongue and not into a foreign language. It can be used to translate incoming correspondence and to determine the content of documents. |
| Multidoc | Multidoc is a 'virtual library', i.e. it contains all the information electronically accessible by electronic means from the library itself. Its purpose is to provide access to information, both internal and external. |
| Multiterm | Multiterm is the terminology-management software adopted by the Commission's translation service. It was developed by the Trados company and is used for running terminology databases and for retrieving terminology. |
| Optical character recognition and speech recognition | The translation service has optical-recognition software which is used for scanning non-electronic documents and for filing purposes, so that such documents can be translated with the help of Translator's Workbench. Speech-recognition software is used in particular by translators used to the dictaphone and by translators unwilling or unable to use a keyboard. |
| Poetry | Software used for the electronic transmission of translation files (original text, worksheets, reference documents). |
| Word-processing | The first computer tool to revolutionise the work of translators. At the Commission, Microsoft Word software has a virtual monopoly on word-processing. |

## List of abbreviations used

| | |
|---|---|
| CFSP | Common Foreign and Security Policy |
| COREPER | Committee of Permanent Representatives |
| DG | Directorate-General |
| DPT | Délégation permanente des traducteurs [Standing Delegation of Translators] |
| EAEC/Euratom | European Atomic Energy Community |
| ECSC | European Coal and Steel Community |
| ECU | European Currency Unit |
| EEC | European Economic Community |
| EMU | Economic and Monetary Union |
| JECL | Abbreviation formed from the names of the streets enclosing the building: Joyeuse entrée, Cortenbergh and Loi. |
| JMO | Jean Monnet building |
| OECD | Organisation for Economic Cooperation and Development |
| OEEC | Organisation for European Economic Cooperation |
| OJ | Official Journal |
| SMLT | Medium- and Long-Term Translation Service |
| UN | United Nations Organisation |

# Abbreviations for Commission departments

| General service departments | |
|---|---|
| JRC | Joint Research Centre |
| COMM | Directorate-General for Communication |
| EAS | European Administrative School |
| EPSO | European Personnel Selection Office |
| ESTAT | Eurostat |
| OLAF | European Anti-Fraud Office |
| OP (formerly OPOCE) | Publications Office of the European Union |
| SG | Secretariat-General |
| **Internal service departments** | |
| BUDG | Directorate-General for Budget |
| BEPA | Bureau of European Policy Advisers |
| DIGIT | Directorate-General for Informatics |
| OIB | Office for Infrastructure and Logistics in Brussels |
| OIL | Office for Infrastructure and Logistics in Luxembourg |
| SCIC | Directorate-General for Interpretation |
| PMO | Office for Administration and Payment of Individual Entitlements |
| ADMIN | Directorate-General for Personnel and Administration |
| IAS | Internal Audit Service |
| SJ | Legal Service |
| DGT | Directorate-General for Translation |
| **External Relations** | |
| TRADE | Directorate-General for Trade |
| DEV | Directorate-General for Development |
| ELARG | Directorate-General for Enlargement |
| AIDCO | EuropeAid Cooperation Office |
| ECHO | Directorate-General for Humanitarian Aid |
| RELEX | Directorate-General for External Relations |

| Policy departments | |
|---|---|
| ECFIN | Directorate-General for Economic and Financial Affairs |
| AGRI | Directorate-General for Agriculture and Rural Development |
| COMP | Directorate-General for Competition |
| EAC | Directorate-General for Education and Culture |
| EMPL | Directorate-General for Employment, Social Affairs and Equal Opportunities |
| ENTR | Directorate-General for Enterprise and Industry |
| TREN | Directorate-General for Energy and Transport |
| ENV | Directorate-General for the Environment |
| TAXUD | Directorate-General for Taxation and Customs Union |
| JLS | Directorate-General for Justice, Freedom and Security |
| MARKT | Directorate-General for the Internal Market and Services |
| MARE | Directorate-General for Maritime Affairs and Fisheries |
| REGIO | Directorate-General for Regional Policy |
| RTD | Directorate-General for Research |
| SANCO | Directorate-General for Health and Consumers |
| INFSO | Directorate-General for the Information Society and the Media |

# Language abbreviations

| | |
|---|---|
| BG | Bulgarian |
| CS | Czech |
| DA | Danish |
| DE | German |
| EL | Greek |
| EN | English |
| ES | Spanish |
| ET | Estonian |
| FI | Finnish |
| FR | French |
| GA | Irish |
| HU | Hungarian |
| IT | Italian |
| LA | Latin |
| LT | Lithuanian |
| LV | Latvian |
| MT | Maltese |

| | |
|---|---|
| NL | Dutch |
| PL | Polish |
| PT | Portuguese |
| RO | Romanian |
| SK | Slovak |
| SL | Slovenian |
| SV | Swedish |

# Glossary

Certain definitions may be amended following
the entry into force of the Lisbon Treaty

| Term | Definition |
|------|-----------|
| *Acquis communautaire or Community acquis* | This expression denotes 'the European Union as it currently exists', i.e. the full set of rights and obligations common to all its Member States. The *acquis communautaire* includes all European legislation and treaties, declarations and resolutions, the international agreements concluded by the European Union and Court of Justice judgments. It also includes action taken by EU governments in the field of justice and home affairs and in connection with the common foreign and security policy. 'Accepting the *acquis*' thus means accepting the European Union as it stands. Applicant countries must accept the *acquis* before joining the European Union and must incorporate Community legislation into their domestic law. |
| *Additional languages* | On 13 June 2005 the Council adopted conclusions concerning the official use of additional languages within the Council and, possibly, within other institutions. Those conclusions relate to languages which are not referred to in Regulation No 1 and whose status is recognised under the Constitution of a Member State on all or part of its territory or which are authorised by law for use as a national language. |
| *Anti-dumping measures* | Measures to combat dumping, i.e. the practice whereby a country sells goods more cheaply abroad than at home. |
| *College of Commissioners* | The European Commission comprises 27 Commissioners, who constitute the College of Commissioners. It meets regularly (generally on Wednesdays) in order to take decisions, in accordance with the Treaties in areas covered mainly by the first pillar (joint policies). Each Commissioner is responsible for one or more areas falling within the Commission's remit. |
| *Comitology* | 'Comitology' refers to an administrative decision-making process involving the consultation of committees. Pursuant to the Treaty establishing the European Community (TEC), the Commission implements legislation at Community level (Article 202 TEC) and is assisted by a committee, in accordance with the procedure known as 'comitology'. Comitology is hence the system used by the Member States to oversee the Commission when the latter adopts implementing measures relating to Community legislation. |
| *Common market* | When it was set up in 1957 the EEC was based on a 'common market': persons, goods and services were to be able to move freely between the Member States as if the latter formed a single country, i.e. without border checks or customs duties. However, it took some time for that point to be reached: customs duties between the EEC countries were not completely abolished until 1 July 1968. Other barriers to trade also took some time to be dismantled and it was not until the end of 1992 that the 'single market' (as it was subsequently called) became a reality. |

| Term | Definition |
|---|---|
| *Community law* | European Union (or Community) law comprises the rules of law upon which the European Union (EU) is founded and the rules which it enacts. It is the law of the European Communities, which are one of the constituent parts of the European Union. It also includes cooperation procedures: the common foreign and security policy (CFSP) and police and judicial cooperation in criminal matters (PJCCM).<br><br>A distinction is made between primary Community or original legislation (comprising the various Treaties) and secondary legislation (see definition below) – the body of laws adopted by the Community institutions in accordance with those Treaties. Lastly, Court of Justice case-law plays an important role as one of the sources of Community law. |
| *'Conversion' course* | A language course which enables translators to learn a foreign language belonging to the same family as a language they already know. |
| *Council of the European Union* | The Council of the European Union ('Council of Ministers' or 'Council') is the European Union's main decision-making body. It meets at the level of Ministers from the Member States and thus constitutes the body representing those States. Its meetings are convened – and their agendas are set – by the Presidency. The Council sits in a total of nine different formations bringing together the appropriate ministers from the Member States: general affairs and external relations; economic and financial affairs; employment, social policy, health and consumers; competition; cooperation in the field of justice and home affairs (JHA); transport, telecommunications and energy; agriculture and fisheries; the environment; education, youth and culture. The EU countries take it in turn to hold the Council Presidency for a six-month period. Council decisions are prepared by the Committee of Permanent Representatives of the Member States (COREPER), assisted by working parties comprising officials from the Member States' civil services.<br><br>The Council performs legislative and budgetary tasks jointly with Parliament. It is the main institution responsible for taking decisions relating to the common foreign and security policy (CFSP) and for coordinating economic policies (intergovernmental approach). It is also the holder of executive power, which it generally delegates to the Commission. In the vast majority of cases the Council takes its decisions on a proposal from the Commission and in co-decision with the European Parliament. Depending on the area concerned, it takes decisions by a simple majority, by a qualified majority or unanimously – although qualified-majority voting is the most widely used (in matters relating to agriculture, the single market, the environment, transport, employment, health, etc.). |
| *Directorate-General* | The staff of the main European institutions (Commission, Council and Parliament) are divided into a number of departments known as directorates-general (DG), which are responsible for specific tasks or policy areas. Each DG is headed by a director-general (sometimes also abbreviated to 'DG'), who runs the DG in administrative terms. |

| Term | Definition |
|------|-----------|
| *European Commission* | The Commission – a politically independent collegiate institution – embodies and protects the European Union's general interests. Since it has a virtually exclusive right of initiative as regards legislative instruments, the Commission is regarded as the driving force behind European integration. In connection with EU policies it prepares – and also implements – the legislative instruments adopted by the Council and the European Parliament. The Commission also has powers of implementation, management and supervision. It plans and implements joint policies, it implements the budget and it runs Community programmes. As the 'guardian of the treaties' it also ensures that European legislation is applied.<br><br>The Commission is appointed for a five-year term by the Council acting by a qualified majority in agreement with the Member States. It is a subject to a vote of appointment by the European Parliament, to which it is answerable. The College of Commissioners is assisted by an administration comprising Directorates-General and specialist departments, the staff of which are split mainly between Brussels and Luxembourg. |
| *European Parliament* | The European Parliament is the assembly of the representatives of EU citizens, who since 1979 have been elected by direct universal suffrage. Parliament has 785 members, distributed between the Member States by reference to their population. In most areas the Parliament shares legislative power with the Council of Ministers, in particular through the co-decision procedure. It shares budgetary power with the Council in adopting the annual budget, making it enforceable through its President's signature and overseeing it implementation. Parliament oversees the policy of the European institutions, in particular that of the Commission. It can give or withhold approval for the designation of the Commission's members and it has the power to dismiss the Commission as a body by means of a motion of censure. It also exercises a power of control over the EU's activities by means of the written and oral questions it can put to the Commission and the Council. Furthermore, Parliament can set up temporary committees and committees of inquiry whose remit is not necessarily restricted to the activities of the Community institutions but can extend to examining the action taken by the Member States in implementing Community policies. |
| *Intergovernmental Conference* | Negotiations between the governments of the EU Member States for the purpose of amending the Community Treaties. |
| *Interinstitutional procedure* | The procedure to be followed when documents are sent from one European institution to another. |
| *International Court of Justice* | Based in The Hague (Netherlands), the International Court of Justice is a UN body set up in 1946 for the purpose of settling international legal disputes. |
| *Interservice consultation* | Procedure in the course of which a number of Commission departments express their opinion on a particular subject. |
| *Language system* | Rules governing the use of languages within the European Union and its institutions. |
| *Machine translation* | Computer software which enables a text to be translated automatically. |

| Term | Definition |
| --- | --- |
| *Non-procedural languages* | At the Commission, all official languages other than English, French and German are non-procedural languages.<br><br>In the legislative process, draft texts are initially submitted in the three procedural languages. Once the Commission has taken a decision on the basis of the three language versions (and one or more additional language versions, if required), the final text is immediately translated into the non-procedural languages and sent to the other EU institutions for consideration and approval. |
| *Official languages* | 'The official languages and the working languages of the institutions of the European Community shall be Bulgarian, Czech, Danish, Dutch, English, Estonian, Finnish, French, German, Greek, Hungarian, Irish, Italian, Latvian, Lithuanian, Maltese, Polish, Portuguese, Romanian, Slovak, Slovenian, Spanish and Swedish.' (Article 1 of Council Regulation No 1 of 1958). These are the languages used by the institutions to communicate with the outside world. |
| *Procedural languages* | For reasons of efficiency, not all the working languages can be used systematically. Pursuant to Article 6 of Regulation No 1, the institutions of the European Union may stipulate in their rules of procedure which of the languages are to be used in specific cases.<br><br>The Commission has designated three procedural languages (English, French and German) in which documents must be available when the Commissioners meet to discuss and take decisions. Draft internal documents which are to be neither published nor forwarded to other Community institutions are also customarily drawn up in one of these languages. Depending on the matter being dealt with (for example, if it concerns a particular Member State), other language versions may be required. |
| *Relay translation* | Working method used when direct translation between source language and target language is not possible: the text is first translated into a 'relay' or 'pivot' language and then into the target language or languages. |
| *Reviser* | Translator whose job is to check the quality of a translation. |
| *Secondary Community legislation* | Secondary community legislation comprises the sources of Community law defined in Article 249 of the EC Treaty: regulations (the equivalent at Community level of national laws: they lay down the rules directly applicable in each Member State); directives (which have an original legal status: addressed to all the Member States or sometimes to just some of them, they lay down mandatory objectives but in principle allow the Member States to decide what means to employ, within a specified deadline); decisions (mandatory for a restricted number of addressees), and recommendations and opinions (which are not binding on the Member States to which they are addressed, although the European Court of Justice takes the view that a recommendation may serve to interpret national or Community law). Secondary legislation is by far the most abundant kind of law. Most secondary legislation stems from the European Union's first pillar. |
| *Source language* | Language from which a translator translates. |

| Term | Definition |
|------|------------|
| *Taiex*<br>*(Technical Assistance and*<br>*Information Exchange)* | The Technical Assistance and Information Exchange programme (TAIEX) provides short-term assistance for institutions relating to the adoption and implementation of the *acquis communautaire*.<br><br>TAIEX assistance is intended for applicant countries, for acceding countries as part of the pre-accession strategy and the screening process, for the ten new Member States and for the countries of the Western Balkans. Amongst other things, TAIEX helps with the translation of legislation and provides expert databases and information concerning the alignment of legislation. |
| *Target language* | Language into which a translator translates. |
| *Treaty languages* | The treaty languages are the ones in which primary legislation (treaties and acts of accession) is drawn up. |
| *Two-way translation* | Term used to denote translation carried out not only into but also out of the translator's mother tongue. |
| *Working languages* | Working languages may be defined as the languages used within the institutions. As provided for in Article 1 of Council Regulation No 1, the official languages are also the European Union's working languages. |

# Iconography

Below we indicate the holders of rights in documents reproduced, together with the source or place of conservation.

We have made every effort to contact rights holders, but we were unable to locate a few.

For further information, please contact:

European Commission
Directorate-General for Translation — Unit 02
B-1049 Brussels
E-mail: DGT-02-SECRETARIAT@ec.europa.eu

| Page | Source used or place of conservation Copyright holder |
|---|---|
| 7 | Photo: Łukasz Kunka |
| 9 | European Commission – Archives |
| 15 | European Commission – Audiovisual Service |
| 18 | European Commission – Archives |
| 21 | European Commission – Directorate-General for Translation– Unit 02 |
| 26 | European Commission – Archives |
| 27 | Photo: William Fraser |
| 28 | Photo: Vaidotas Pateckas |
| 29 | Photo: Vaidotas Pateckas |
| 34 | European Commission – Directorate-General for Translation– Unit 02 |
| 35 | European Commission – Audiovisual Service |
| 39 | European Commission – Directorate-General for Translation– Unit 02 |
| 44 | European Commission – Extract of *Commission en direct n° 466* |
| 65 | European Commission – Directorate-General for Translation– Unit 02 |
| 79 | Photo: Klaus Meyer-Koeken |

# Bibliography

European Commission, *The European Commission 1958-1972, History and memories of an institution*,
Office for Official Publications of the European Communities, 2007

Coulmas, F., *A language policy for the European Community: Prospects and Quandries*,
Mouton de Gruyter, Berlin-New York, 1991.

Fosty, A., *La langue française dans les institutions communautaires de l'Europe*,
Conseil de la langue française, Quebec, 1985.

Labrie, N., *La construction linguistique de la Communauté européenne*,
collection «Politique Linguistique» n° 1, Honoré Champion, Paris, 1993.

Truchot, C., *Le plurilinguisme européen: théories et pratiques en politique linguistique*,
Champion-Slatkine, Paris-Geneva, 1994.

Wagner, E., Bech, S. and Martínez, J. M., *Translating for the European Union Institutions*,
St Jerome Publishing, Manchester, 2002.

JECL staircase

A GREAT DEAL of other information concerning the Directorate-General for Translation is available on the Internet via the Europa server (http://ec.europa.eu/dgs/translation/index_fr.htm)

A paper version of this publication is available in English, French and German. An electronic version is available on the EU Bookshop website (http://bookshop.europa.eu/eubookshop/index.action).

The Directorate-General for Translation (DGT) makes information concerning the European Union accessible to all EU citizens by translating it into their languages. It also provides language services and advice to the European Commission. This document pays tribute to the work performed by DGT's staff since the 1950s. It describes the various stages leading to the establishment of the DGT, looks back over DGT's achievements and considers the challenges which lie ahead of it.

European Commission

**Translation at the European Commission – a history**

Luxembourg: Office for Official Publications of the European Communities

2010 — 79 p. — 21 x 25,5 cm

ISBN 978-92-79-08849-0
doi: 10.2782/16417

## How to obtain EU publications

Publications for sale:

- via EU Bookshop (http://bookshop.europa.eu);

- from your bookseller by quoting the title, publisher and/or ISBN number;

- by contacting one of our sales agents directly.

You can obtain their contact details on the Internet (http://bookshop.europa.eu) or by sending a fax to +352 2929-42758.

Free publications:

- via EU Bookshop (http://bookshop.europa.eu);

- at the European Commission's representations or delegations.

You can obtain their contact details on the Internet (http://ec.europa.eu) or by sending a fax to +352 2929-42758.

Превод

Překlady

Oversættelse

Übersetze

Μετάφραση

Translation

Traducción

Tõlkimine

Kääntämine

Traduction

Aistriúchá

Fordítás